Mayan Terracottas

Irmgard
Groth Kimball

Mayan Terracottas

Introduction
by
José Dane
Kimball

Frederick A. Praeger, *Publishers*
New York

BOOKS THAT MATTER

Published in the United States of America in 1961
by Frederick A. Praeger, Inc., Publishers
64 University Place, New York 3, N.Y.

The plates for the black-and-white illustrations were produced by
Graphische Kunstanstalt Kuenstle, Tuebingen; the color plates were
produced by Graphische Kunstanstalt Carl Ruck, Stuttgart.
Printing and binding by Ensslin-Druck, Reutlingen, Germany

We wish to thank the Instituto Nacional de Antropología e Historia, Mexico, as well as the museums and private collectors, for giving their kind permission to photograph the art objects reproduced in this book. We are especially obliged to the eminent archeologist Rafael Orellana Tapia for his contribution to the explanatory notes on the photographs. His recent death is an irreparable loss.

I. G. K.

The Great Priests – the Halac Uinic – reigned for a thousand years. They invented a calendar, studied astronomy, and created a world of abstractions and symbols, developing a culture that became outstanding in world history. But at the end of the sacred millenium, the gods left the earth, and their temples in the forests were deserted. The priests lost their hold on the people, and warriors took over. The rise and decline of Maya culture of the 'old empire' is tied to the rise and fall of theocracy.

The delicate figurines of the classic period evoke the Mayan thought and artistry. This small sculpture, elegant and expressive, is at the same time significant of the history of American culture in showing the details of everyday life. This refined work continued into the 'new empire', which corresponds to the Nahuatl-Toltec invasion of the Post-Classic Horizon, and it is believed that terracotta figurines were still being made at the time of the Spanish conquest. This belief is based on the Nahuatloide elements in some of the figurines, as for instance the horizontal lines found in the repesentations of throne temples, which are typical of Toltec architecture.

Terracotta figurines of the Jaina type have been found in various sites of the Maya domain: from the region of the Tuxtlas at the Gulf to Honduras, at Palenque, on the island of Jaina, at Jonuta, Chixoy, Mayapán in the area of the Usumacinta, at Lubaatun in Belice, in the Petén, and at Alta Vera Paz in Guatemala.

The most fruitful site of all has been the archaeological cemetery of Jaina, a small island separated from the coast of Campeche by a narrow branch of the Gulf of Mexico. The Maya name 'Jaina' means 'the house on the sea'. In the 16th century, the Franciscan father Diego de Anda, second bishop of Yucatán, described the impression of the first Occidentals: "In the midst of the ocean, but not far from shore, rises a building like a quadrangular tower of white limestone with steps. It resembles a fortress, but is a temple, on the walls of which are represented, hewn in stone, serpents and other animals. In the background there is an altar, and upon it an immense idol with two lions or tigers stained with blood biting into its flanks. At the bottom is a serpent over 40 feet long, which devours a lion. Everything is well carved in fine stone."

The temples were destroyed, as was the custom, and the débris used with other building materials in new constructions. Visitors today see nothing but a landscape of mounds rising from the waters, once the trapping grounds of Francis Drake and of pirates.

The Mexican Government has organized successful excavations on the island. The archaeologists found tombs everywhere, not far below the surface, as the land is not far above sea-level. The bodies were buried in big clay vessels covered by clay tripods. The skeletons were found lying on one side, knees close to the chest, arms crossed over them, a pose typical in American burials, and often depicted in codici. The terracotta figurines, as religious offerings, were put next to jewellery such as rings, ear ornaments, knives of rock crystal, obsidian or bone, necklaces, mosaics, fishing hooks, points, spindles, plates and cups. Jade beads are often found between the maxillary bones or fallen into the skull. This would indicate a practice like the oriental one of putting toll money for the last journey into the mouth of the deceased. The bones show traces of vermilion. Evidently, the bodies were painted with the sacred colour, the colour of blood, the most precious offering.

In each tomb there were one or more terracotta figurines. They were placed in the hands of the deceased, and the higher his rank, the more figurines he would hold.

The tradition of terracotta sculpture goes far back to the beginnings of Meso-American history. In the pre-classic period a high level of artistic technique had been reached in modelling and firing. The Americans of those days had solved the problems of terracotta-making centuries before our time.

During the classic period, the technique of casting in moulds was developed, making it possible to produce many copies of the same model. As a result of the variation in technique, we may classify the figurines as: hand modelled, cast in moulds, or a combination of both. The pictures in this book show examples of all three techniques, as explained in the captions. Some of the figurines are hollow and were used as whistles, rattles, or both.

On most of the terracotta figures, one can still see traces of paint. Unfortunately, the physical conditions were not favourable for preserving the colour, and most of it disappeared. The Mayas lived in a colourful world: they painted their bodies, their buildings, their ceramics, and they painted their dead. They preferred red, and also used blue, yellow, white, green and black.

Predominant among the figurines is the representation of the sun god, the high priests and dignitaries on their thrones with headdresses of Quetzal plumes, ear ornaments, breast plates, collars, bracelets and anklets, and often dressed in elegant cloaks. And the world of aristocratic women is represented too, a world reminiscent of Asiatic luxury, with a pageantry of servants in reverent attitudes. Now and then one finds a figurine representing a simple peasant woman, with a jar on her head or a child on her hip; but probably these are representations of a fertility goddess.

The faces are realistic and expressive, while the bodies are modelled with freedom and vigour, and the resulting effect is monumental and forceful.

The Jaina figurines reveal the architecture, ornaments, physical types and skull deformation, costume, jewellery, furniture, ritual paraphernalia and weapons. The statuettes also represent ball players, warriors, dancers and musicians, and a whole court of buffoons and dwarfs; there are monkeys, jaguars, rabbits, owls, dogs and turtles. In short, the whole Mayan world is disclosed to us, with its refined balance between realism and poetic freedom.

Where were the figures made which are found in the tombs of Jaina? There are no archeological 'rubbish heaps' on Jaina that would indicate a settlement or ceramic workshop. Do the figurines represent courtiers or the dead? What does the recurring theme of the lustful old man and the young woman symbolize? What is the meaning of the glyphs and why do dwarfs hide between the folds of a woman's cloak? Jaina is a treasure island of reality and mystery.

X

CHICHEN ITZA

MAYAPAN

COBA

TULUM

JAINA

UXMAL KABAH

SAYIL LABNA

EDZNA

JONUTA

USUMACINTA

CALAKMUL

NAACHTUN

UAXACTUN

PIEDRAS NEGRAS

PALENQUE

NAKUM

NARANJO

TONINA

TIKAL

TAYASAL

ALTAR DE SACRIFICIOS

YAXCHILAN

SEIBAL

LUBAANTUN

CHIXOY

ALTA VERAPAZ

QUIRIGUA

MOTAGUA

COPAN

Jacobo Rodriguez

Notes:

[1] The main garment of the men was a loincloth, ranging from a simple belt of cotton cloth with an apron in front, to a wide kilt-like band.

[2] The frontal-occipital skull deformation was obtained by binding the head of a newborn child between two boards. This was an aristocratic practice and was always a sign of high rank.

[3] For the Maya the ideal profile had a continuous line from the forehead to the nose. This was obtained by a bridgelike addition to the nose placed between the brows, probably held in place by resin.

[4] The typical dress of the Maya woman consisted of a circular cotton-cloth, pulled over the head and worn as a shirt, the "kub". The "pic" was a wrap-around skirt.

[5] The hollow figurines were cast in moulds, the solid ones modelled by hand; the details were made of pasted-on clay beads or coils, the technique being called "appliqué" (pastillaje). The three techniques were frequently combined. The heads were mostly moulded.

Plates

HÖCHSTER PRIESTER UND WÜRDENTRÄGER „HALACH UINIC",
auf einem mit Hieroglyphen geschmückten Thron sitzend. Er trägt
einen kunstvoll gearbeiteten Kopfputz, der einen phantastischen Vogel
mit ausgebreiteten Flügeln und Schwanz aus langen Federn darstellt,
dessen Kopf die Maske der Sonnengottheit „Kinich Ahau" bildet.
Prächtiger Ohrenschmuck, eine zweireihige Halskette aus viereckigen
Jade-Platten mit kreisrunden Sonnenscheiben verziert und der Lendenschurz „ex"[1] mit luxuriöser Schärpe vervollständigen seine Bekleidung.
Blaue Farbreste. In der Form hergestellt. Höhe: 19,3 cm. Sammlung:
Diego Rivera.

HIGH PRIEST AND DIGNITARY "HALACH UINIC", seated on a throne
decorated with glyps. He wears an elaborate head-dress in the shape
of a fantastic bird with outspread wings and a long feathered tail. The
bird's head is formed by the mask of the sun God "Kinich Ahau".
Earplugs, a two-stringed necklace of rectangular jade plaques with
three solar disks forming the breastplate, and the "ex[1]" or loin cloth
with an intricately decorated front piece like an apron, make up the
costume of this High Priest.
Traces of blue paint. Molded. Height: 19.3 cm. Collection: Diego
Rivera.

GRAND PRETRE ET HAUT DIGNITAIRE «HALACH UINIC», assis sur
un thrône orné de hiéroglyphes. Il porte une coiffure élaborée avec art,
et qui représente un oiseau phantastique aux ailes déployées et à queue
de longues plumes et dont la tête forme la masque du dieux du
soleil «Kinich Ahau». De splendides ornements aux oreilles, un collier
composé de deux rangs de plaques en jade carrées, décorées de disques solaires et le pagne «ex» garni d'une luxueuse écharpe, complètent son costume.
Traces du couleur bleue – Figurine faite au moule. Hauteur: 19,3 cm.
Collection: Diego Rivera.

GRAN SEÑOR «HALACH UINIC». Está sentado en un trono decorado
con jerogli-ficos. Lleva sobre la cabeza un elaborado tocado en forma
de ave fantástica, con las alas y la cola de largas plumas extendidas. La
cabeza del ave está formada con la máscara de la deidad solar «Kinich
Ahau». Vistosas orejeras, dos sartales de placas de jade con tres discos
solares, que forman el pectoral y el «ex» o braga[1] de lujoso colgante al
frente, completan la indumentaria del Gran Señor.
Muestra restos de pintura azul. Hecho en molde. Altura: 19,3 cm.
Colección: Diego Rivera.

[1] vide p. XIV

VORNEHME DAME in befehlender Haltung, das drücken die auf den Knien aufgestützten Hände aus. Zeichen ihrer vornehmen Herkunft ist der deformierte Schädel (frontal-okzipital)[2]. Mittelscheitel und gestutzter Haarschopf über der Stirn ist die typische Frisur. Ein Nasenaufsatz[3] verlängert den Nasenrücken. Sie trägt Ohrenpflöcke, Armreifen und eine Halskette aus kugel- und röhrenförmigen Perlen, deren lange Enden fast bis zum Schoß reichen. Die Kleidung besteht aus dem Obergewand „kub" und dem Rock „pic"[4].
Geringe Reste von blauer Bemalung. In der Form hergestellt, handmodelliert und mit plastischen Auflagen versehen. Höhe: 13,3 cm. Privatsammlung.

LADY in commanding posture, as denoted by the position of her hands on her knees. The frontal-occipital[2] deformation of her head indicates her high rank. Her hair is parted in the middle, a forelock falling on her forehead. The bridge of the nose is extended artificially to make a continuous line from the forehead to the tip of the nose[3]. Her jewelry consists of circular earplugs, bracelets and a necklace of large tubular and spherical beads. Her garments are the "kub", a shirt, and the "pic" or skirt[4].
Scant traces of blue and white paint. Molded, hand-modeled and appliquéd. (Gingerbread technique). Height: 13.3 cm. Private Collection.

DAME DISTINGUÉE, dans l'attitude de l'ordre, ce qu'expriment ses mains posées à plat sur ses genoux. Sa haute origine est attestée par la déformation frontale-occipitale du crâne[2]. La raie au milieu et la mèche de cheveux taillée en carré sur le front représentent la coiffure typique. Un ornement nasal[3] prolonge l'arête nasale. Elle porte des disques d'oreilles, des bracelets et un collier de perles rondes et tubulaires, dont les extrémités lui descendent presque jusqu'aux genoux. Son costume se compose de la blouse «kub» et de la jupe «pic»[4].
Quelques traces de couleur bleue. Figurine faite au moule, modelée à la main suivant la technique du pastillage[5]. Hauteur: 13,3 cm. Collection privée.

GRAN SEÑORA. En actitud de mando, por tener las manos sobre las rodillas. La deformación craneana fronto-occipital[2] acusa su alto linaje. El peinado está partido al centro con guedeja al frente. Tiene un aditamento en el nacimiento de la nariz[3]. Se ornamenta de orejeras circulares, pulseras y un sartal de grandes cuentas tubulares y esféricas. Como indumentaria tiene el «kub» o camisa circular y el «pic» o falda[4].
Conserva escasos restos de pintura azul y blanca. Hecha en molde, a mano libre y con pastillaje. Altura: 13,3 cm. Colección: Particular.

KRIEGER, in ehrerbietiger Haltung, das drücken die über der Brust gekreuzten Arme aus. Auf dem Kopf trägt er ein feines Baumwoll-geflecht und ein Diadem aus kreisförmigen Ornamenten, als Brust-schmuck eine Muschel mit hängender Perle. Die Wangen sind ta-tauiert, an Mundwinkeln und Kinn sind zu Knötchen verheilte Haut-einschnitte. Er ist bekleidet mit dem Lendenschurz „ex" und einer breiten Mittelschärpe.

Weiße Farbreste. In der Form hergestellt, handmodelliert und mit pla-stischen Auflagen versehen.[5] Höhe: 18 cm. Sammlung: Museo Reg. de Campeche, Camp.

WARRIOR, in reverent attitude, as revealed by his crossed arms. On his head an intricate braiding of cords and a diadem of circular orna-ments. His breastplate is a shell with a pearl. The nose has been extended, the cheeks are tattooed, and there is beaded scarification at the corners of the mouth and on his chin. He wears an "ex", or loin-cloth with a wide apron.

Traces of white paint. Molded, hand-modeled and appliquéd.[5] Height: 18 cm. Collection: Museo Reg. de Campeche, Camp.

GUERRIER, dans une pose révérencielle exprimée par les bras croisés sur la poitrine. Il porte sur la tête un fin ouvrage tressé de coton et un diadème d'ornements circulaires, et en guise de pectoral un coquillage auquel pend une perle. Il a les joues tatouées et des nodosités prove-nant d'incisions aux commissures des lèvres et sur le menton. Il est vêtu du pagne «ex» et d'une large ceinture.

Traces de peinture blanche. Faite au moule, modelée à la main d'après a technique du pastillage.[5] Hauteur: 18 cm. Collection: Musée Régiona de Campeche, Camp.

GUERRERO. En actitud reverencial, como lo indica la posición de los brazos cruzados. Lleva en la cabeza un delicado trenzado de cordón y una diadema de ornamentos circulares. Porta un pectoral de concha de la que pende una perla. Tiene aditamento en el nacimiento de la nariz, tatuaje en las mejillas y escoriaciones en las comisuras de los labios y en la barbilla. Se viste con el «ex» o braga con ancha banda al frente.[5]

Conserva restos de pintura blanca. Hecho en molde, a mano libre y con técnica de pastillaje[5]. Altura: 18 cm. Colección: Museo Reg. de Cam-peche, Camp.

JUNGFRAU. Die hohe Stellung, die den Frauen eingeräumt wurde, läßt vermuten, daß bei den Mayas das Matriarchat herrschte. In diesem Figürchen ist der Reiz weiblicher Zartheit und Anmut ausgedrückt. Die Schädeldeformation bezeugt ihren Rang. Wahrscheinlich hielt sie einen Fächer in der rechten Hand. Die Pose läßt vermuten, daß eine Tänzerin dargestellt ist.
Wahrscheinlich der Kopf in der Form hergestellt, alles übrige hand-modelliert. Höhe: 8 cm. Sammlung: Dr. Kurt Stavenhagen.

YOUNG GIRL. The high estimation in which the Maya held their women has led to the belief that a matriarchy existed. This figurine is full of feminine grace and charm. The skull deformation shows her high rank. She had probably been holding a fan in her right hand. Her pose is that of a dancer.
The head probably molded, body and details hand-modeled and appliquéd. Height: 8 cm. Collection: Dr. Kurt Stavenhagen.

VIERGE. La haute considération dont jouissait la femme maya laisse supposer que le matriarchat régnait chez les Mayas. Tout le charme de la délicatesse et de la grâce féminines se trouve exprimé dans cette figurine. La déformation cranienne atteste son rang. Elle tenait pro-bablement dans la main droite un éventail. On devine à la pose qu'il s'agit d'une danseuse.
Tête probablement faite au moule. Tout le reste modelé à la main. Hauteur: 8 cm. Collection: Dr. Kurt Stavenhagen.

DONCELLA. La elevada consideración de la mujer maya invita a pen-sar en el matriarcado. Esta figurilla expresa con delicadeza el encanto y la gracia femeninas. La deformación craneana acredita su rango. Probablemente tuvo un abanico en la mano derecha. La figurilla parece ser una bailarina.
La cabeza probablemente hecha en molde. El cuerpo y los accesorios a mano libre y con técnica de pastillaje. Altura: 8 cm. Colección: Dr. Kurt Stavenhagen.

4

HÖCHSTER PRIESTER UND WÜRDENTRÄGER „HALACH UINIC". Er sitzt auf einem Thron mit herabhängenden Beinen, eine bei den Mayas wenig übliche Haltung. Die Frisur besteht aus Haarbüscheln mit Bändern und Rosetten geschmückt, darüber sitzt ein Kopfputz aus Federn. Der Schädel ist deformiert. Er trägt einen kostbaren Brustschmuck aus mehreren Perlenschnüren und Arm- und Fußreifen. Der Lendenschurz „ex" ist mit einer Schärpe, mit Bändern und Fransen verziert.
Blaue und weiße Farbreste. Handmodelliert und mit plastischen Auflagen versehen. Höhe: 23 cm. Privatsammlung.

HIGH PRIEST AND DIGNITARY "HALACH UINIC", seated on a throne, his legs hanging down, an exceptional feature. His hair is done up in locks tied in cords and decorated with rosettes, topped by a panache of plumes. Skull deformation. He wears a large collar of several beaded strings, cuffs on his wrists and anklets. The "ex" or loincloth has dangling sashes and tassels.
Blue and white paint traces. Hand-modeled and appliquéd. Height: 23 cm. Private Collection.

GRAND PRÊTRE ET HAUT DIGNITAIRE «HALACH UINIC». Il est assis sur un thrône, les jambes pendantes, attitude peu répandue chez les Mayas. Sa chevelure est séparée en touffes de cheveux ornées de rubans et de rosettes sur lesquelles est posé un panache de plumes. Le crâne est déformé. Il porte un précieux pectoral fait de plusieurs rangs de perles et des bracelets aux bras et aux pieds. Son pagne «ex» est agrémenté d'une écharpe, de rubans et de franges.
Traces de peinture bleue et blanche. Figurine modelée à la main d'après la technique du pastillage. Hauteur: 23 cm. Collection privée.

GRAN SEÑOR «HALACH UINIC». Sentado en un trono presenta la característica excepcional de tener las piernas colgando. Su cabellera está adornada con mechones de pelo adornados con cordones y rosetones y rematada por un penacho de plumas. Muestra deformación craneana. Porta un gran pectoral de varios sartales de cuentas, así como pulseras y ajorcas. Lleva el «ex» de bandas colgantes y flecos. Conserva restos de pintura blanca, azul y negra. Modelado a mano libre con técnica de pastillaje. Altura: 23 cm. Colección: Particular.

WÜRDENTRÄGER in befehlender Haltung. Der betont deformierte Schädel ist geschoren. Er trägt einen Schnurr- und Kinnbart, eine Mode, die bei den Mayas nicht sehr gebräuchlich war. Kreisförmiger Ohrenschmuck, Halsband aus runden Scheiben mit Anhänger und Armreifen sind der übliche Schmuck. Dazu trägt er einen breiten Lendenschurz „ex". Es fehlt der Kopfschmuck aus Federn, der abnehmbar war.

In der Form hergestellt, handmodelliert und mit plastischen Auflagen versehen. Höhe 16,5 cm. Sammlung: Carlos Pellicer.

DIGNITARY in commanding posture. His extraordinarily deformed head is shaven. He has moustaches and a beard, an unusual fashion with the Maya. His plume panache, which probably was removable, is missing. He wears circular earplugs, a strand of disks with a pendant, wristlets and a wide loincloth "ex".

Molded, hand-modeled and appliquéd. Height: 16.5 cm. Collection: Carlos Pellicer.

DIGNITAIRE, dans une attitude impérative. La déformation du crâne rasé est très prononcée. Il porte une moustache et une barbe, mode peu répandue chez les Mayas. Les ornements circulaires des oreilles, le collier de perles rondes avec pendantif et les bracelets sont les bijoux habituels. Il est vêtu d'un large pagne «ex». Il lui manque sa coiffure de plumes, qui était sans doute amovible.

Figurine faite au moule et modelée à la main suivant la technique du, pastillage. Hauteur: 16,5 cm. Collection: Carlos Pellicer.

SEÑOR. Su actitud es de mando. Presenta una pronunciada deformación craneana. Tiene la cabeza rapada, lleva bigotes y barbilla, lo que es excepcional. Le falta el tocado de plumas que seguramente era desmontable. Porta orejeras circulares, sartal de discos y pinjante pulseras y el «ex» en la cintura.

Hecho en molde, a mano libre y con técnica de pastillaje. Altura: 16,5 cm. Colección: Carlos Pellicer.

SONNENGOTT „KINICH AHAU". Er sitzt auf einem Altar. Sein Kopfschmuck stellt einen Vogel mit ausgebreiteten Flügeln dar. Kopf und Schwanz werden in der Mitte ersetzt durch eine Reihe von übereinander aufgebauten Masken, die die Sonne repräsentieren. Die großen viereckigen Augen des Gottes, der Kinnbart und das Flechtwerk an den Seiten beziehen sich auf das Symbol des Tages „kin". Er trägt einen Brustschmuck aus drei Schüren von viereckigen Platten aus Jade, und in den Händen hält er das Manequi-Zepter. Angedeutet ist ein Schultertuch aus Federn.
In der Form hergestellt. Höhe: etwa 15 cm. Sammlung: Museo Nacional de Antropología, México.

SUN GOD "KINICH AHAU", seated on an altar. His head-dress represents a bird with outspread wings. A series of masks symbolizing the sun, placed one above the other, forms the bird's head and tail. His eyes are large rectangles. His beard and the braiding at the sides of his face are related to the day sign "kin". He wears a large collar of three strands of rectangular jade beads, and in his hand he holds the "manikin-scepter". His back is covered with a plume cape.
Molded. Height: about 15 cm. Collection: Museo Nacional de Antropología, Mexico.

DIEU DU SOLEIL «KINICH AHAU». Il est assis sur un autel. Sa coiffure représente un oiseau aux ailes déployées. La tête et la queue de celui-ci font place vers le milieu à une série de masques posés les uns sur les autres qui symbolisent le soleil. Les grands yeux rectangulaires du dieu, la barbe et les tressages latéraux se rapportent au symbole du jour «kin». Il porte sur la poitrine un pectoral composé de trois rangs de plaques de jade carrées et tient à la main le sceptre «manequi». On devine sur ses épaules une cape de plumes.
Figurine faite au moule. Hauteur: environ 15 cm. Collection: Musée National d'Anthropologie, Mexico.

DIOS SOLAR «KINICH AHAU». Está sentado en un altar. Lleva como tocado un ave con las alas extendidas. La cabeza y la cola del ave están representadas por una serie de mascarones superpuestos identificados con el sol. Los ojos son grandes y cuadrangulares. La barbilla y los trenzados laterales del dios están relacionados con el símbolo del día «kin». Porta un gran pectoral de tres sartales de placas cuadrangulares de jade y en las manos sostiene el cetro-manequí. Le cubre la espalda un lienzo formado de plumas.
Fabricado en molde. Altura: 15 cm. Colección: Museo Nacional de Antropología, México.

TÄNZER. Der kultische Tanz nahm einen wichtigen Platz ein. In prächtiger Aufmachung, zum eintönigen Klang der Flöten und Tamburine, bestimmten die Tänzer den Rhythmus Mesoamerikas. Die Figur trägt einen hohen konischen Kopfputz aus einem bauschigen Material auf dem deformierten Schädel, sie ist mit einem Diadem aus Perlen oder Jadesteinen, mit Ohrgehänge, Brustschmuck aus runden Scheiben und Arm- und Fußreifen aus Röhrenperlen geschmückt. Auf dem Rücken ist ein großer Fächer aus Federn befestigt. Lendenschurz „ex" mit Gürtel aus Perlen und einer breiten, verzierten Mittelschärpe.
In der Form hergestellt. Höhe: 15,3 cm. Sammlung: Dr. Kurt Stavenhagen.

DANCER: Ritual dance was a prominent feature of the Mayan life. In festive custume, to the monotonous beating of drums and the squealing of flutes, the dancers moved in the patterns of Central-American rhythm. On his deformed head, the figurine wears a conic headdress of a ruffled material topped by an animal head. He also wears a diadem of jade beads, circular ear ornaments with pendants, bracelets and anklets of tubular beads. A plume fan is fastened to his back, and his loincloth of tubular beads ends in a very elaborate apron.
Molded. Height: 15.3 cm. Collection: Dr. Kurt Stavenhagen.

DANSEUR. Les danses rituelles occupaient une place prépondérante dans la civilisation maya. Dans de splendides atours et au son monotone des flûtes et des tambourins, les danseurs fixèrent le rythme d'Amérique Centrale. Le danseur porte sur son crâne déformé une haute coiffure conique faite d'un matériau bouffant. Il est paré d'un diadème de perles et de jades, de pendants d'oreilles, d'un pectoral de plaques circulaires et de bracelets de perles tubulaires aux bras et aux pieds. Un grand éventail de plumes est fixé sur son dos. Le pagne «ex» est retenu par une ceinture de perles et enrichi d'une large écharpe décorée.
Figurine faite au moule. Hauteur: 15,3 cm. Collection: Dr. Kurt Stavenhagen.

DANZANTE. La danza ritual ocupaba un lugar prominente. En lujosos y monumentales atavíos, al son monótono de flautas y tamboriles, los danzantes marcan la arquitectura del ritmo Mesoamericano. La figurilla lleva un alto tocado cónico de material abullonado, rematado por una cabeza de animal. Se adorna con diadema de cuentas de jade, orejeras circulares de colgajos, pectoral con sartales de discos, pulseras y ajorcas de canutos. En la espalda porta un gran abanico de plumas y una banda muy elaborada forma el «ex».
8   Fabricado en molde. Altura: 15,3 cm. Colección: Dr. Kurt Stavenhagen.

PRIESTER. Er trägt einen Spitzhut mit breiter, hochgeschlagener Krempe. Die Spitze wird gekrönt von einer Schleife oder Blume. Der besonders hohe Nasenaufsatz betont das klassische Maya-Profil. Er hat einen kleinen Kinnbart und ist mit Ohrenscheiben und einem dicken schalähnlichen Halsband geschmückt. Er trägt ein kurzärmeliges blaues Kleid „buc". Das Blau ist die Farbe der Priester. An der rechten Hand sind nur noch die Schnüre, an denen die Weihrauchtasche hing.
Gut erhaltene Bemalung. Handmodelliert und mit plastischen Auflagen versehen. Der Kopf vermutlich in der Form hergestellt. Höhe: 17,3 cm. Sammlung: Museo Nacional de Antropología, México.

PRIEST, wearing a pointed wide-brimmed hat topped by a flower or a bow. The ideal Mayan profile is achieved by the addition to the nosebridge. He has a small beard, earplugs and a scarf around his neck. He is covered with a „buc", a short sleeved blue cloak, blue being the color for the priests. All that is left of an incense bag, in his right hand, is the cords.
The paint is well preserved. The head is probably molded, the body and details were hand-modeled and appliquéd. Height: 17.3 cm. Collection: Museo Nacional de Antropología, Mexico.

PRÊTRE. Il porte un chapeau pointu à large bord relevé. La pointe est couronnée d'un noeud ou d'une fleur. L'ornement nasal particulièrement élevé met en valeur le profil maya. Il porte une petite barbiche et est paré de disques d'oreilles et d'un épais collier semblable à une écharpe. Il est vêtu d'une tunique bleue à manches courtes «buc». Le bleu était la couleur sacerdotale. Il ne reste plus que les cordons du sac d'encens qu'il tenait dans sa main droite.
Tête probablement faite au moule, tout le reste modelé à la main et suivant la technique du pastillage. Hauteur: 17,3 cm. Collection: Musée National d'Anthropologie, Mexico.

SACERDOTE. Sobre la cabeza porta un sombrero de ancha ala y alta copa rematada por un moño o una flor. Acusa un aditamento en el nacimiento de la nariz, que viene a formar el clásico perfil maya. Tiene barbilla. Se adorna con orejeras y collar de gruesa banda. Cubre el cuerpo con un «buc» o vestido de manga corta de color azul, color propio de los sacerdotes. En la mano derecha sostiene el cordel de la bolsa de copal, la que está rota. La pintura está bien conservada.
La cabeza probablemente hecha en molde. El cuerpo y los accesorios modelados a mano libre y aplicados mediante pastillaje. Altura: 17,3 cm. Colección: Museo Nacional de Antropología, Mexico.

BALLSPIELER. Sein Kopfputz ist aus Baumwolle und hat hinten am Nacken eine Schutzvorrichtung. Er ist mit einem „yugo" (jochförmiger Gürtel) gegürtet, ein sehr umstrittener Gegenstand aus prähispanischer Zeit, und weist uns auf den möglichen Gebrauch desselben hin. Er läßt vermuten, daß der „yugo" – wahrscheinlich aus Holz – als Schutz diente und zugleich, um die Schläge des Balles beim rituellen Spiel zu erwidern. Eine große Schließe in Vogelform ist ein Hinweis auf die wahrscheinliche Verwendung dieser sog. „palmas", die in der Kunst der Mayas äußerst selten vorkommen, dagegen sehr häufig in den Golfkulturen anzutreffen sind.

Rote und weiße Farbreste. In der Form hergestellt, handmodelliert und mit plastischen Auflagen versehen. Höhe 17,5 cm. Privatsammlung.

BALL PLAYER. His cotton head-dress includes a protective device at the back. Skull deformation. Around his waist, he wears a "yugo" one of the most debated Pre-Spanish artifacts. This figurine suggests that the "yugo" – probably made of wood – was used as a protection and to make the ball rebound in the ceremonial game. The "yugo" of this figurine has a large buckle in front, in the shape of a bird, and perhaps offers an explanation for the use of the so-called "palmas", rare in Mayan Art, but frequently found in the Gulf cultures.

Traces of red and white paint. Molded, hand-modeled and appliquéd. Height: 17.5 cm. Private Collection.

JOUEUR DE BALLE. Sa coiffure est en coton et possède à l'arrière un dispositif protecteur. Il est ceint d'un «jugo» (ceinture en forme de joug), objet fort discuté de l'époque pré-hispanique, et dont on devine ici l'emploi qui en était fait. Il servait à la fois à protéger le joueur des coups de balle et à renvoyer ceux-ci au cours des jeux rituels. Un grand fermoir en forme d'oiseau laisse supposer à quoi servait probablement ce dénommé «palmas» que l'on trouve fort rarement dans l'art maya, mais par contre très fréquemment dans les civilisations du Golfe.

Traces de couleur rouge et blanche. Faite au moule, modelée à la main et d'après la technique du pastillage. Hauteur: 17,5 cm. Collection privée.

JUGADOR DE PELOTA. Lleva un tocado de algodón con protector en la parte posterior. Presenta deformación craneana. Muestra en la cintura el uso del «yugo», uno de los objetos prehispánicos más discutidos. La figurilla hace suponer que, el «yugo», probablemente de madera, servía como defensa y para contestar los golpes de la pelota en el juego ritual. El «yugo» presenta al frente un gran broche en forma de ave y parece explicar un uso de las llamadas «palmas», piezas excepcionales en el arte maya, pero abundantes en las culturas del Golfo.

Conserva restos de pintura roja y blanca. Hecho en molde, a mano libre y con pastillaje. Altura: 17,5 cm. Colección: Particular.

BALLSPIELER. Seinen Kopf bedeckt ein riesiger Turban aus ge-
bauschter Baumwolle, der auf der Rückseite zwei steife Streifen hat,
die den Spieler gegen Stöße des massiven Gummiballes schützen soll-
ten. Auf dem linken Unterarm trägt er einen Schutzriemen. Sein Schädel ist deformiert und ein Nasenaufsatz verlängert den Nasenrücken.
Der Kopf ist wahrscheinlich in der Form hergestellt, alles übrige handmodelliert und mit plastischen Auflagen versehen. Höhe: 28 cm. Sammlung: Museo Nacional de Antropología, México.

BALL PLAYER. His deformed head is covered by an enormous turban
of ruffled cotton material with two stiff ribbons in the back for protection against the solid rubber ball used in the game. Also his left arm is
protected by a ban. His nose is noticeably prolonged to the forehead.
The head is probably molded, the body and details hand-modeled and
appliquéd. Height: 28 cm. Collection: Museo Nacional de Antropología,
Mexico.

JOUEUR DE BALLE. Il porte sur la tête un gigantesque turban de coton
bouffant, muni à l'arrière de deux bandes raides, destiné à protéger
le joueur des coups de la balle de caoutchouc massif. Il a sur l'avant-
bras gauche une lanière protectrice. Son crâne est déformé et l'arête
nasale est prolongée artificiellement. La tête a probablement été faite
au moule, tout le reste modelé à la main et suivant la technique du
pastillage.
Hauteur: 28 cm. Collection: Musée National d'Anthropologie, Mexico.

JUGADOR DE PELOTA. Su cabeza está cubierta por un turbante
monumental hecho de algodón abullonado, que lleva en su parte
posterior dos franjas o tiras que sirven como defensa para los golpes
de la pelota de hule sólido, que se usaba en el juego. En el antebrazo
izquierdo tiene un protector. Muestra deformación craneana y un aditamento sobre el nacimiento de la nariz.
La cabeza probablemente hecha en molde. El cuerpo y los accesorios
modelados a mano libre y aplicados mediante pastillaje. Altura: 28 cm.
Colección: Museo Nacional de Antropología, México.

HOHER PRIESTER „HALACH UINIC". Er trägt einen hohen und kunstvollen Kopfschmuck mit einem steifen Federbusch, den ein Band mit Rosetten zusammenhält. Hinter dem Kopf und dem Rücken hat er fächerförmige Verzierungen aus gefaltetem Papier. Schnüre halten die Mundmaske. Ihn schmücken kreisförmige Ohrpflöcke, ein reich mit Perlen und Jadesteinen verzierter Brustschmuck, Arm- und Fußreifen. Der Lendenschurz „ex" ist mit Perlen und Borten bestickt. Er trägt Sandalen. In der linken Hand hält er die mit Quasten versehene Weihrauchtasche mit „copal". Der „copal" ist ein aromatisches Harz, das bei den heiligen Riten verbrannt wurde.
Die Figur ist eine Rassel. In der Form hergestellt. Höhe: 20 cm. Sammlung: Museo Reg. de Campeche, Camp.

HIGH PRIEST "HALACH UINIC". He wears a high and ornamental head-dress of stiff plumes tied together with a band of rosettes. The back of his head, as well as his shoulders, is adorned with big fans of pleated paper. He wears circular earplugs, a mouth-mask held in place by cords, and a collar made of several strands of pearls and jade beads. He is attired in an "ex" that ends in an apron, in a wide bead-embroidered belt, bracelets, anklets and sandals. In his left hand he holds a tasseled copalbag–copal being an aromatic resin burnt at sacred rites. The figurine is a rattle. Molded. Height: 20 cm. Collection: Moseo Reg. de Campeche, Camp.

GRAND PRÊTRE «HALACH UINIC». Sa tête est coiffée d'un couvre-chef savamment élaboré et orné d'un bouquet de plumes raides attachées par un ruban garni de rosettes. Derrière la tête et sur le dos, il porte des ornements en éventail, faits de papier plissé. Des cordons tiennent le masque de la bouche. Il est paré d'ornements d'oreilles circulaires, d'un pectoral richement décoré de perles et de jades, et de bracelets aux bras et aux pieds. Le pagne «ex» est brodé de perles et de galons. Il est chaussé de sandales, et tient dans sa main gauche un sac à encens garni de pompons, renfermant du «copal», résine aromatique que l'on brûlait au cours des jeux rituels. Figurine-crécelle faite au moule.
Hauteur: 20 cm. Collection: Musée Régional de Campeche, Camp.

GRAN SACERDOTE «HALACH UINIC». Lleva un alto y lujoso tocado formado de penachos de plumas rígidas, anudados con una banda de rosetones. Tanto en la parte posterior de la cabeza, como en la espalda tiene adornos, de papel plegado, en forma de abanico. Se ornamenta de orejeras circulares, de una máscara bucal sostenida por cordones y de un pectoral de varios sartales de cuentas de perlas y jades. Se cubre con el «ex» de banda colgante al frente y ceñido por un ancho cinturón bordado de cuentas. Porta pulseras, ajorcas y sandalias. En la mano izquierda sostiene la bolsa de copal con flecos. El copal es una recina aromática que se quemaba en los ritos sagrados.
Figurilla-sonaja, hecha en molde. Altura: 20 cm. Colección: Museo Reg. de Campeche, Camp.

ALTER KRIEGER, der ein Kleid „buc" aus Baumwolle anhat, das typische Gewand der Militärkaste. Die Brust schmückt eine große viereckige Platte. Auf der Nasenwurzel ist ein Aufsatz zu sehen. In der rechten Hand hält er einen runden, mit Quaste und breiter Borte verzierten Fächer.

Blaue und rote Farbreste. Die Figur ist eine Okarina und in der Form hergestellt. Höhe: 15 cm. Sammlung: Museo Nacional de Antropología, México.

OLD WARRIOR, attired in a "buc", a cotton dress of the military caste decorated with a large rectangular breast plate. On his brow a nasal addition or a scarification. In his right hand he holds a round fan decorated with a wide fringe and a tassel.

Traces of blue and red paint. The figure is an ocarina. Molded. Height: 15 cm. Collection: Museo Nacional de Antropología, Mexico.

VIEUX GUERRIER, vêtu de la tunique «buc», vêtement caractéristique de la caste militaire. Il porte sur la poitrine une grande plaque rectangulaire, et à la racine du nez, l'ornement nasal habituel. Il tient dans sa main droite un éventail rond, garni d'une large bordure et d'un pompon. Ocarina faite au moule. Traces de peinture bleue et rouge. Hauteur: 15 cm. Collection: Musée National d'Anthropologie, Mexico.

ANCIANO GUERRERO. Cubre su cuerpo con el «buc» o vestido de algodón, propio de la milicia. Porta aditamento en el nacimiento de la nariz. Se adorna con un pectoral cuadrangular. En la mano derecha empuña un abanico orlado con una borla.

Conserva restos de pintura azul y roja. Figurilla-ocarina, hecha en molde. Altura: 15 cm. Colección: Museo Nacional de Antropología, México.

KRIEGER, der auf einer Bank liegt und sich in einem Rundschild, der ihm als Spiegel dient, bewundert. Der runde Schild ist die im nördlichen Hochland gebräuchliche Form, und diese Tatsache verleiht der Figur den Charakter einer späteren Epoche. Seine Haartracht ist ein kompliziertes Geflecht aus Haarbüscheln, die durch Röhrchen gezogen sind, und Bändern. Das Diadem ist charakteristisch für den Krieger Mesoamerikas. Der deformierte Schädel, der Nasenaufsatz und der Spitzbart unterstreichen seinen Rang. Die gekreuzten Arme sind auf einer gerollten Decke aufgestützt.

Rote und weiße Bemalung. Handmodelliert und mit plastischen Auflagen versehen. Höhe: 17 cm. Privatsammlung.

WARRIOR, reclinging on a bench and looking at himself in a round shield as in a mirror. The shape of the shield is the usual for the Northern Plateau, which assigns the piece to a late period. His hair is dressed intricately in locks pulled through tubular beads and braided with cords. The diadem is typical for the Central-American warrior. High rank is indicated by the skull deformation and the addition to the nose. The crossed arms rest on a rolled blanket.

Traces of red and white paint. Hand-modeled and appliquéd. Height: 17 cm. Private Collection.

GUERRIER, couché sur un banc et s'admirant dans un bouclier circulaire qui lui sert de miroir. La forme circulaire est la forme propre au Haut-Plateau, ce qui rattache cette figurine à une époque récente de la civilisation maya. Sa coiffure est un ouvrage compliqué de touffes de cheveux passées dans des tubes et entrelacées de rubans. Le diadème est une propriété du guerrier d'Amérique centrale. La déformation cranienne, la prolongation artificielle du nez et la barbiche attestent son rang. Ses bras eroisés reposent sur une couverture roulée.

Peinture rouge et blanche. Figurine faite à la main et suivant la technique du pastillage. Hauteur: 17 cm. Collection privée.

GUERRERO. Está recostado sobre un banquillo y se admira en una rodela a manera de espejo. La rodela circular es de la forma propia del altiplano, lo que da a la pieza un carácter tardío. Lleva en la cabeza el peinado de mechones de cabellos separados por canutos y trenzados con cordones. El adorno de diadema es característico del guerrero mesoamericano. Se observa deformación craneana y aditamento en el nacimiento de la nariz. El «ex» está anudado con grueso ceñidor. Los brazos cruzados se apoyan en una manta enrollada.

Conserva restos de pintura roja y blanca. Modelado a mano libre con técnica de pastillaje. Altura: 17 cm. Colección: Particular.

TÄNZER. Er hat einen großen, kreisförmigen Kopfschmuck aus Papier, dessen seitliche Flügel Mauerzinnen ähneln und der gehalten wird von drei Federbündeln und einem Stirnband. Die Schädeldeformation ist frontal-okzipital und bilobular. Letzteres war wenig gebräuchlich bei den Mayas, im Gegensatz zu anderen Völkern an der Golfküste. Er trägt Ohrenscheiben mit langen Anhängern, eine Halskette aus verschiedenartigen Perlen und einen Brustschmuck, der aus einer Jadeplatte besteht mit dem eingravierten Bild einer schielenden Gottheit. Das Schielen galt als göttliche Eigenschaft. Der rockähnliche Lendenschurz ist mit gefransten Bändern und Borten verziert.

In der Form hergestellt, handmodelliert und mit plastischen Auflagen versehen. Höhe: 25 cm. Sammlung: Museo Nacional de Antropología, México.

DANCER. His large, circular head-dress resembles at either end the merlons of a battlement. It is fastened with a band around his head and decorated with three bundles of feathers in the shape of birds' tails. His skull deformation is frontal-occipital and bilobular, the latter being rare among the Maya, while typical of other peoples of the Gulf. He wears large circular ear ornaments with long pendants, a necklace of beads of varied shapes supporting a rectangular breastplate of jade on which the image of a cross-eyed deity is engraved. Squinting was considered a divine quality. The loincloth is a wide fringed and frilled skirt-like band.

Molded, hand-modeled and appliquéd. Height: 25 cm. Collection: Museo Nacional de Antropología, Mexico.

DANSEUR. Il a sur la tête une vaste coiffure circulaire de papier, dont les ailes latérales rappellent des créneaux et qui est maintenue par trois plumets et un bandeau. La déformation cranienne est frontale-occipitale et bilobulaire. Cette dernière particularité était peu fréquente chez les Mayas, à l'inverse des autres peuples de la côte du Golfe. Il porte aux oreilles des disques à longues pendeloques, un collier de perles variées et un pectoral fait d'une grande plaque de jade gravée d'une divinité bigle. Le strabisme était une propriété divine. Le pagne en forme de jupe est orné de rubans à franges et de galons.

Figurine faite au moule, modelée à la main et suivant la technique du pastillage. Hauteur: 25 cm. Collection: Musée National d'Anthropologie, Mexico.

DANZANTE. Lleva un gran tocado circular de papel con laterales en forma de almenas, sostenido por tres atados de plumas en forma de cola de ave y una banda alrededor de la cabeza. Presenta deformación craneana fronto-occipital y bilobular, esta última poco usual entre los mayas, pero característica de otros pueblos del Golfo. Porta orejeras. Un sartal de cuentas y pendientes sostiene un pectoral, probablemente una placa de jade, en la que está grabada la cara de una deidad que presenta estrabismo, característica divina. El «ex» es en forma de faldilla con adornos de bandas.

Hecho en molde, a mano libre y con pastillaje. Altura: 25 cm. Colección:
15   Museo Nacional de Antropología, México.

TÄNZER. Ihn kleidet ein Gewand „buc", das vermutlich aus „vainas", den Früchten eines tropischen Baumes, besteht. Wenn die Früchte trocknen, bleiben die Samen lose in den Schoten und begleiten die Bewegungen durch ein rhythmisches Rasseln. Dieser Umstand erlaubt uns die Vermutung, daß diese Figur einen Tänzer darstellt. Ferner trägt er eine Halskrause, die von einer dicken Kordel gehalten wird. Der deformierte Schädel ist kahl und es fehlt der Kopfschmuck, der vermutlich abnehmbar war.

Blaue Farbreste. Der Kopf wahrscheinlich in der Form hergestellt, alles übrige handmodelliert und mit plastischen Auflagen versehen. Höhe: 28 cm. Sammlung: Ehem. Staatl. Museum für Völkerkunde, Berlin.

DANCER. His dress is probably made of pods from a tropical tree. When dry, the loose seeds rattle to the movements of the dance. He wears a ruff tied by a thick cord, and his shaved skull, exaggeratedly deformed, lacks the plume headdress which, presumably, was removable. A marked bridge-like addition to the nose.

Traces of blue paint. The head was probably molded, the body and details hand-modeled and appliquéd. Height: 28 cm. Collection: Ehem. Staatl. Museum für Völkerkunde, Berlin.

DANSEUR. Il est vêtu d'un «buc», vêtement fait probablement de «vainas», fruits d'un arbre tropical. Lorsqu'ils sèchent, les graines se détachent à l'intérieur des gousses et accompagnent chaque mouvement d'un cliquetis rythmique. Ce vêtement nous permet de supposer qu'il s'agit ici d'un danseur. Il porte encore une collerette attachée par une grosse cordelière. Le crâne est déformé et chauve. Il manque probablement la coiffure qui devait être amovible.

Traces de peinture bleue. Tête probablement faite au moule, tout le reste modelé à la main suivant la technique du pastillage. Hauteur: 28 cm. Collection: Ehem. Staatl. Museum für Völkerkunde, Berlin.

DANZANTE. Se supone que se trata de un danzante porque lleva un «buc» o vestido formado por lo que parecen ser vainas, el fruto de un árbol tropical. Al secarse dicho fruto las semillas quedan sueltas en el interior y que suena como sonaja, marcando el ritmo. Lleva una gorguera sostenida por un grueso cordón. Muestra exagerada deformación craneana, la cabeza rapada y aditamento en el nacimiento de la nariz. Le falta el tocado de plumas, que era desmontable.

Conserva restos de pintura azul. La cabeza probablemente fabricada en molde. El cuerpo y los accesorios hechos a mano libre y con técnica de pastillaje. Altura: 28 cm. Colección: Ehem. Staatl. Museum für Völkerkunde, Berlin.

WEIBLICHER KOPF. Die hohe und kunstvolle Haartracht endet in einem dicken Haarknoten und ist mit einem Diadem aus viereckigen Platten und Tierkopf – vermutlich eine Schildkröte – verziert. Der deformierte Schädel unterstützt die monumentale Wirkung. – Auf der Stirn ist ein künstlicher Aufsatz angebracht.
In der Form hergestellt. Höhe: 7 cm. Sammlung: Museo Regional de Villahermosa, Tab.

FEMALE HEAD. The high and elaborate head-dress emphasizes the skull deformation. It ends in a thick tuft of hair and is ornamented with a diadem of rectangular plaques, from the center of which protrudes the head of an animal, probably a tortoise. The forehead bears an addition to the nose. Large earplugs.
Molded. Height: 7 cm. Collection: Museo Regional de Villahermosa, Tab.

TETE DE FEMME. La haute et savante coiffure se termine par un gros chignon. Elle est ornée d'un diadème fait de plaques rectangulaires et d'une tête d'animal, sans doute une tortue. La déformation du crâne souligne l'effet monumental. Sur son front est fixé l'ornement destiné à obtenir le profil maya.
Faite au moule. Hauteur: 7 cm. Collection: Musée Régional de Villahermosa, Tab.

CABEZA FEMENINA. Lleva un alto y delicado peinado terminado en una bola de cabellos y ornamentado con una diadema de cuadrángulos que tienen en el centro la cabeza pequeña de un animal, al parecer una tortuga. Presenta deformación craneana y aditamento en el nacimiento de la nariz.
Hecha en molde. Altura: 7 cm. Colección: Museo Regional de Villahermosa, Tab.

VORNEHME DAME. Die hohe Haartracht wird von geflochtenen Bändern geschmückt und gehalten. Die Schädeldeformation ist betont. Auf der Nasenwurzel hat sie einen kleinen Aufsatz und an den Lippen, am Kinn und auf dem Nasenrücken sind Knötchen, die durch Hauteinschnitte entstehen. Ohrpflöcke, Brustschmuck, Armreifen und ein über Schultern und Kleid fallender Mantel, vervollständigen die Kleidung.

Gut erhaltene Bemalung. Die Figur ist eine Pfeife. In der Form hergestellt, handmodelliert und mit plastischen Auflagen versehen. Die Figur hat die seltene Höhe von 41 cm. Sammlung: Hon. Robert Woods Bliss.

LADY. Her high head-dress is decorated and held in place by braided cords. Extraordinary skull deformation. On the brow over her nose, the, usual addition; on the chin, the lips and the nose-ridge beaded scarifications. Earplugs, a breastplate and wristlets are her jewelry. A cloak over her shoulders covers her.

The paint is well preserved. The figurine is a whistle, molded, handmodeled and appliquéd. Its exceptional height: 41 cm. Collection: Hon. Robert Woods Bliss.

DAME DE NOBLE ORIGINE. Sa haute coiffure est garnie et maintenue par des rubans tressés. La déformation cranienne est très accusée. A la racine du nez, elle porte un petit ornement nasal et sur les lèvres, le menton et l'arête nasale, des nodosités produites par des incisions. Des disques aux oreilles, un pectoral et des bracelets ainsi qu'un manteau sur les épaules et une robe complètent sa tenue.

Peinture bien conservée. Figurine-sifflet, faite au moule et modelée suivant la technique du pastillage. Hauteur assez exceptionnelle de: 41 cm. Collection: Hon. Robert Woods Bliss.

GRAN SEÑORA. Lleva un alto tocado sostenido y adornado por cordones trenzados. Presenta deformación craneana muy pronunciada, un aditamento en al nacimiento de la nariz y escoriacicnes en el filo de la nariz, en los labios y en la barbilla. Porta pectoral y pulseras. Un manto le cae sobre la espalda.

La pintura está bien conservada. Figurilla-silbato, hecha en molde, a mano libre y con pastillaje. Tiene la altura excepcional de 41 cm.

Colección: Hon. Robert Woods Bliss.

VORNEHME DAME, in würdevoller Haltung, mit Schädeldeformation. Ein kunstvoller Haarschopf belegt die schlichte, in der Mitte gescheitelte Frisur. Sie schmückt sich mit Ohrpflöcken, einer großen Perlenschnur und Armbändern aus Röhrenperlen. Die Kleidung setzt sich zusammen aus dem Obergewand oder der Bluse „kub" und dem Rock „pic". In der Form hergestellt, handmodelliert und mit plastischen Auflagen versehen. Höhe: 18,5 cm. Sammlung: Museo Nacional de Antropología, México.

DISTINGUISHED LADY, in commanding posture. Her hair is parted simply in the center, a lock falling on the deformed forehead. Her jewelry consists of round earplugs with buttons, a strand of large spherical beads and tubular bead cuffs; her garment is the "kub" and the "pic". Molded, hand-modeled and appliquéd. Height: 18.5 cm. Collection: Museo Nacional de Antropología, Mexico.

DAME DISTINGUÉE, dans une attitude pleine de dignité. Le crâne est déformé. Les cheveux sont partagés par une raie au milieu et cette coiffure sobre est rehaussée par une mèche artistiquement taillée. Elle est parée de disques d'oreilles et d'un grand collier de perles ainsi que de bracelets de perles tubulaires. Son costume se compose de la blouse «kub» et de la jupe «pic». Figurine faite au moule, modelée à la main et suivant la technique du pastillage. Hauteur: 18,5 cm. Collection: Musée National d'Anthropologie, Mexico.

GRAN SEÑORA. En actitud de mando. El sencillo peinado está partido al centro con guedeja al frente. Muestra deformación craneana. Se adorna con orejeras circulares de botón, sartal de grandes cuentas esféricas y pulseras de canutos. Se cubre con el «kub» y el «pic». Hecha en molde, a mano libre y con técnica de pastillaje. Altura: 18,5 cm. Colección: Museo Nacional de Antropología, México.

WEIBLICHE GOTTHEIT, die mit dem Wasser und der Fruchtbarkeit in Beziehung gebracht wird. Ihre Attribute sind der Wasserkrug, den sie auf dem Kopf trägt, und das Kind, das rittlings auf ihren Hüften sitzt. Sie hat Ohrenscheiben, eine Perlenschnur, deren Enden bis auf die Hüften fallen, und Armbänder. Das Obergewand „kub" ist einfach, der Rock „pic" dagegen ist mit Mäander und einer Borte aus Fransen verziert. Daß diese Figur aus einer späteren Zeit stammt, beweisen die Mäander.
Die Figur ist eine Rassel und in der Form hergestellt. Höhe: 16 cm. Sammlung: Stendahl.

FEMALE DEITY related to water and fertility by the water jug on her head and the child carried astride on her hip. Her hair is terraced to frame the face, a forelock is in the middle. She wears earplugs, bracelets and a bead necklace, its ends tied together and reaching down to her waist, over a simple "kub". The "pic" has a border or meandering fret, and frills. The meander indicates a late period.
This figurine is a rattle. Molded. Height: 16 cm. Collection: Stendahl.

DIVINITE FEMININE, se rapportant à l'eau et à la fécondité. Ses attributs sont la cruche d'eau qu'elle porte sur sa tête et l'enfant, assis à califourchon sur ses hanches. Elle est parée de disques d'oreilles, d'un collier de perles dont les bouts tombent jusqu'aux hanches et de bracelets. La blouse «kub» est sobre; la jupe, par contre, est ornée de méandres et d'un galon à franges. Les méandres rattachent cette figure à une époque récente de l'art maya.
La figurine est une crécelle, faite au moule. Hauteur: 16 cm. Collection Stendahl.

DEIDAD. Relacionada con el agua y la fertilidad. Sus atributos son la olla que lleva sobre la cabeza y el infante que lleva a horcadas en la cintura. Está peinada con guedeja al centro. Se adorna con orejeras circulares, sartal de cuentas anudadas al frente y pulseras. El «kub» es sencillo y el «pic» está decorado con greca que termina en un fleco de orlas. La greca evidencia su carácter tardío.
20   Figurilla-sonaja, hecha en molde. Altura: 16 cm. Colección: Stendahl.

HOHER PRIESTER UND WÜRDENTRÄGER „HALACH UINIC", der auf einem Thron sitzt. Der elegante Kopfschmuck besteht aus einem leichten Gestell, das einen Aufbau von Stangen, Bändern, Rosetten und Fransen stützt. Er trägt eine breite, um Nacken und Hals geschlungene und zu einer Schleife gebundene Schärpe, lange, bandartige Ohrgehänge mit Fransen verziert und Baumwollrollen um die Waden. In der Form hergestellt, handmodelliert und mit plastischen Auflagen versehen. Höhe: 13 cm. Sammlung: Museo Nacional de Antropología, México.

HIGH PRIEST AND DIGNITARY "HALACH UINIC", seated on a throne. The elegant head-dress consists of a light framework decorated with rosettes, ribbons and tassels. The usual addition to the nose and a beard typical for old people. The ear ornaments have long pendants with fringes, and the collar is a wide sash tied into a bow overhanging the "ex". The leggings are cotton bands. Molded, hand-modeled and appliquéd. Height: 13 cm. Collection: Museo Nacional de Antropología, Mexico.

GRAND PRETRE ET HAUT DIGNITAIRE «HALACH UINIC», assis sur un thrône. Son élégante coiffure est composée d'une légère armature qui supporte un édifice de bâtons, de rubans, de rosettes et de franges. Il est vêtu d'une large écharpe passée autour de sa nuque et de son cou et qui se termine par un noeud sur les genoux. Il porte de longs pendants d'oreilles semblables à des rubans et garnis de franges et autour des mollets des bourrelets de coton. Figurine faite au moule et modelée à la main d'après la technique du pastillage. Hauteur: 13 cm. Collection: Musée Nat. d'Anthropologie, Mexico.

GRAN SEÑOR «HALACH UINIC». Sentado en un trono. El elegante tocado está armado con un ligero armazón y adornado con barras rematadas por un grueso cordón con adornos circulares y un colgante lateral. Presenta el aditamento usual sobre la nariz. Tiene una barbilla, característica de los ancianos. Las orejeras terminan en flecos y el collar en un moño. Los adornos de los tobillos son rollos de algodón. Hecho en molde, a mano libre y con técnica de pastillaje. Altura: 13 cm.

Colección: Museo Nacional de Antropología, México.

FRAU vornehmer Herkunft mit auffallend starker Schädeldeformation und rechtwinklig ausrasierten Stirn- und Schläfenhaaren. Auf Stirn und Unterlippe sind künstliche Erhöhungen angebracht. Runde Ohrpflöcke, Halskette und spangenähnlicher Brustschmuck und der über den Brüsten beginnende Rock „pic" sind von betonter Einfachheit. In der linken Hand hält sie eine fächerähnliche runde Scheibe aus Palmengeflecht. Der kreuzförmige Ausschnitt ist das Symbol für den Wind „ik".

Die Figur ist eine Okarina. In der Form hergestellt, handmodelliert und mit plastischen Auflagen versehen. Höhe: 22,5 cm. Sammlung: Museo Reg. de Villahermosa, Tab.

LADY aristocrat with pronounced deformation of the head. Her hair is shaved rectangularly around her forehead and temples. Scarifications on her forehead and below her lower lip. Earplugs, a choker and a tubular breast ornament from her unpretentious jewelry. Her simple "pic" is tied above her breasts. She holds a round woven palm disk in her left hand which is perforated in the shape of the wind symbol "ik".

The figurine is an ocarina. Molded, hand-modeled and appliquéd. Height: 22.5 cm. Collection: Museo Reg. de Villahermosa, Tab.

FEMME DE HAUT RANG. La déformation cranienne est très prononcée. Les cheveux sont rasés rectangulairement sur le front et les tempes. Des incisions lui décorent le front et la lèvre inférieure. Elle porte des disques aux oreilles, un collier et un pectoral en forme d'agrafe. Le tout est d'une grande simplicité ainsi que la tunique «pic» qui commence aux seins. Elle tient dans la main gauche une sorte d'éventail en feuilles de palmiers tressées, percé d'une croix qui symbolise le vent «ik».

Ocarina, faite au moule et modelée à la main à la technique du pastillage. Hauteur: 22,5 cm. Collection: Musée Regional de Villahermosa, Tab.

SEÑORA. Con deformación craneana muy notable y la frente rasurada en forma rectangular. Lleva aditamento en la frente y en el labio inferior. Se adorna con orejeras, collar y pectoral. El «pic» muy sencillo cubre desde los senos. En la mano izquierda sujeta lo que parece ser abanico circular tejido de palma con una apertura que representa el símbolo del «ik» o sea el viento.

Figurilla-ocarina. Hecha en molde, a mano libre y con pastillaje. Altura: 22,5 cm. Colección: Museo Reg. de Villahermosa, Tab.

WÜRDENTRÄGER in befehlender Haltung. Er trägt einen Kopfputz aus gewickelten und geflochtenen Baumwollstreifen. Der Schädel ist deformiert, das Gesicht tatauiert und mit einem Nasenaufsatz versehen. Lange Ohrgehänge, ein Halsband aus umeinandergewundenen Baumwollwülsten und geflochtene Armbänder schmücken ihn. Die breite Mittelschärpe vom Lendenschurz „ex" fällt über seine Füße. In der Form hergestellt, handmodelliert und mit plastischen Auflagen versehen. Höhe: 29 cm. Sammlung: Miguel Covarrubias.

DIGNITARY, in commanding posture. Head-dress of elegantly tied and braided cotton bands which hang down his back. Deformed head. Face tattooed and scarified with lines and dots. Nose addition. He wears long ear pendants, a necklace of twisted cotton cords, the ends of which fall over his shoulders, and bracelets of the same material. The broad apron of his "ex" covers his crossed feet. Molded, hand-modeled and appliquéd. Height: 29 cm. Collection: Miguel Covarrubias.

DIGNITAIRE, dans l'attitude de l'ordre. Il porte une coiffure de bandes de coton savamment enroulées et tressées. Le crâne est déformé, le visage tatoué et l'arête nasale prolongée. De longues boucles d'oreilles, un collier fait de bourrelets de coton entrelacés et des bracelets tressés le parent. La grande écharpe médiane du «pagne ex» lui couvre les pieds. Figurine faite au moule et modelée d'après la technique du pastillage. Hauteur: 29 cm. Collection: Miguel Covarrubias.

SEÑOR. En actitud de mando. Lleva un tocado de bandas elegantemente trenzadas con colgante hacia atrás. Señalada deformación craneana. Tiene un tatuaje de lineas y puntos en el nacimiento de la nariz y en las comisuras de los labios. Se adorna de orejeras de largos colgantes triangulares, collar de gruesos cordones retorcidos con colgantes que caen sobre los hombros y una pulsera de cordón trenzado. Un ancho colgajo que forma parte del «ex» cae sobre las piernas. Hecho en molde, a mano libre y con técnica de pastillaje. Altura:

29 cm. Colección: Miguel Covarrubias.

PRIESTER (Ausschnitt). Die Gesichtszüge zeigen das charakteristische Profil der Mayas, das durch den über der Nasenwurzel angebrachten Nasenaufsatz erzielt wurde. Der Nasenrücken wird so bis zur Stirn hinauf verlängert. Er trägt einen Spitzhut mit breiter, hochgeschlagener Krempe. Die Spitze wird gekrönt von einer Blume.
Vergleiche Text zu Tafel 9. Höhe: 17,3 cm. Sammlung: Museo Nacional de Antropología, México.

PRIEST (Detail). His face has the characteristic ideal profile of the Maya, obtained by the addition to the nose between the brows. He wears a pointed wide-brimmed hat topped by a flower.
Cf. comm. plate 9. Red, white and blue paint. Height: 17.3 cm. Collection: Museo Nacional de Antropología, Mexico.

PRÊTRE (Détail). Les traits de son visage représentent le profil maya caractéristique que l'on obtenait en ajoutant à la racine du nez une sorte de «raccord». L'arête nasale était ainsi prolongée jusqu'au front. Il porte un chapeau pointu à large bord relevé et couronné à son sommet d'une fleur.
Voir le commentaire de la planche 9. Hauteur: 17,3 cm. Collection: Musée Nat. d'Anthropologie, Mexico.

SACERDOTE (Detalle). Sus facciones caracterizan el típico perfil maya, cuyo ideal se logra con el aditamento en el nacimiento de la nariz. Porta un sombrero de ancha ala y alta copa rematada por una flor.
Véase texto de la plancha 9. Está pintado de rojo, blanco y azul. Altura: 17,3 cm. Colección: Museo Nacional de Antropología, México.

FRAU (Ausschnitt). Sie ist von vornehmer Herkunft, hat Schädel-deformation und einen Nasenaufsatz. Die Haare sind in der Mitte ge-scheitelt und sitzen glatt am Kopf an. Auf der Brust sind Reste einer Perlenschnur.
In der Form hergestellt, handmodelliert und mit plastischen Auflagen versehen. Höhe: 22 cm. Sammlung: Museo Nacional de Antropología, México.

WOMAN (Detail). Her hair is parted simply in the middle and pulled straight back from her forehead: this is deformed to indicate her high rank. She wears earplugs and some remaining beads of a necklace.
Molded, hand-modeled and appliquéd. Height of the entire figurine: 22 cm. Collection: Museo Nacional de Antropología, Mexico.

FEMME (Détail). Elle est de noble origine comme le prouvent la dé-formation de son crâne et la prolongation de l'arête nasale. Ses cheveux sont coiffés plats et partagés par une raie au milieu. On voit sur sa poitrine les restes d'un collier de perles.
Faite au moule, modelée à la main et suivant la technique du pastillage. Hauteur: 22 cm. Collection: Musée National d'Anthropologie, Mexico.

SEÑORA (Detalle). Su peinado está partido al frente. Presenta defor-mación craneana y aditamento en el nacimiento de la nariz. Conserva restos del collar de cuentas.
Hecha en molde, a mano libre y con pastillaje. Altura: (de la figura entera) 22 cm. Colección: Museo Nacional de Antropología, México.

ALTER MANN MIT FRAU. Der Greis trägt einen Federhelm mit einer Rosette und einen gewebten Brustschmuck mit Fransen und Quasten. Die Schärpe vom Lendenschurz „ex" ist gestickt und reich verziert. Beide schmücken sich mit Ohrgehänge, Halskette und Armbändern. Der Kopfputz der Frau ist aus einem bauschigen Material und mit Rosetten, Bändern und Quasten versehen. In der linken Hand hält sie einen Fächer. Sie ist mit der Bluse „kub", dem Rock „pic" und einem langen Umhang bekleidet.
Die Figur hat weiße Farbreste und ist eine Rassel. In der Form hergestellt. Höhe: 16 cm. Privatsammlung.

OLD MAN AND WOMAN. He wears a helmet of stiff feathers with a rosette at the side and pendants. His round breastplate suspended by a wide necklace is woven and decorated with tassels. The loincloth has an elaborately embroidered apron. The woman's head-dress is of a ruffled material adorned with ribbons and rosettes. She wears earplugs with pendants, strands of beads and wristlets. In her left hand she holds a round fan. She is dressed in a "kub", a "pic", in this case a fringed skirt, and a long cape.
This figurine is a rattle, molded. Traces of white paint. Height: 16 cm. Private collection.

VIEIL HOMME ET SA FEMME. Le vieillard porte un casque de plumes garni d'une rosette et un pectoral à franges et à pompons. L'écharpe du pagne «ex» est brodée et richement décorée. Les deux personnages sont parés de pendants d'oreilles, de colliers et de bracelets. Le chapeau de la femme est fait d'un matériau bouffant et agrémenté de rosettes, de rubans et de glands. Elle porte dans la main gauche un éventail et elle est vêtue de la blouse «kub», et de la jupe «pic» ainsi que d'une longue cape.
Traces de peinture blanche. Figurine-crécelle, faite au moule. Hauteur: 16 cm. Collection privée.

ANCIANO Y SEÑORA. El anciano lleva un casco de plumas, rosetón lateral y colgantes. Se adorna con un ancho collar y un pectoral tejido en forma circular y con flecos. El «ex» tiene larga banda muy elaborada. La señora lleva un tocado de material abullonado y ornamentado con bandas y rosetones. Porta orejeras de dos colgantes, sartas de cuentas y pulseras. En la mano izquierda sostiene un abanico. Se cubre con el «kub» y el «pic» y con un largo manto.
Conserva restos de pintura blanca. Figurilla-sonaja, hecha en molde. Altura: 16 cm. Colección: Particular.

JUNGFRAU. Das lose herabfallende Haar läßt den deformierten Schädel deutlich werden. Der sparsame Schmuck besteht aus Ohrpflöcken, Armreifen und dem Rest einer Perlenschnur. Der Gegensatz zwischen dem sorgsam modellierten Gesicht und der Einfachheit der plastischen Wiedergabe des Körpers, dessen Gliedmaßen sich dem Gesamtvolumen unterordnen, ist charakteristisch. Völlig unbekleidete Maya Terrakotten sind selten.

Handmodelliert und mit plastischen Auflagen versehen. Der Kopf ist vermutlich in der Form hergestellt. Höhe: 22 cm. Privatsammlung.

YOUNG GIRL in the nude. Her flattened forehead is noticeable under her plain hair falling loosely over her shoulders. She is modestly bejeweled with earplugs and wristlets, only two beads being left of her necklace. The well modeled and expressive face forms a characteristic contrast with the simple body, where only the principal forms of the limbs have been indicated. Complete nudity is rare in Mayan clay figures.

The head was probably molded, the body and details were handmodeled and appliquéd. Height: 22 cm. Private Collection.

VIERGE. Ses cheveux tombent souplement autour de sa tête et soulignent la déformation cranienne. Elle est parée de disques d'oreilles, de bracelets et d'un collier de perles dont il ne reste plus que des traces. Le contraste est frappant entre la richesse de l'expression du visage soigneusement travaillé et l'extrême sobriété dans la facture du corps dont les membres ont été stylisés à l'extrême. La nudité complète est rare dans la céramique maya.

Tête probablement faite au moule. Tout le reste à la main suivant la technique du pastillage. Hauteur: 22 cm. Collection privée.

DONCELLA. Figurilla desnuda. Presenta deformación craneana, pulseras y restos del sartal de cuentas. La cabellera suelta cae sobre la espalda y el frente. Es muy característico el cuidadoso detalle del rostro en contraste con la extrema simplicidad del cuerpo, cuyos miembros se reducen a la expresión del volúmen. La desnudez completa es excepcional en la cerámica maya.

Está pintada de rojo y negro. La cabeza probablemente fabricada en molde. El cuerpo y los accesorios hechos a mano libre y con técnica de pastillaje. Altura: 22 cm. Colección: Particular.

FRAU UND ZWERG. Sie trägt einen hohen Kopfputz aus gedrehten, geflochtenen und gesteiften Baumwollwülsten, die durch einen Hut mit breiter Krempe hindurchgezogen sind und oben heraushängen. Schädeldeformation, eine künstliche Erhöhung auf der Stirn, Perlenschnur und Armbänder bezeugen ihre hohe Stellung. Ein über Schultern und Rücken fallender Mantel rahmt die Gestalt eines alten, zwerghaften Mannes ein, der zwischen ihren Beinen hockt.
Blaue, rote und weiße Bemalung. In der Form hergestellt, handmodelliert und mit plastischen Auflagen versehen. Höhe: 23 cm. Sammlung: Dr. Kurt Stavenhagen.

WOMAN AND DWARF. Her headress is made of twisted, braided and striped cotton cords pulled through a wide-brimmed hat with a zigzag edge placed at a slant high on top of her hair. The ends of the cotton cords hang down from the crown of the hat. Her skull is deformed, and she has a bulge on her forehead. The bulge, as well as the pearl necklace and cuffs, shows her high rank. A long coat covers her shoulders and frames the figure of an old dwarf squatting between her legs.
Traces of blue, red and white paint. Molded, hand-modeled and appliquéd. Height: 23 cm. Collection: Dr. Kurt Stavenhagen.

FEMME ET NAIN. La femme porte une haute coiffure faite de bourrelets de cotons raides entrelacés qui passent à travers un chapeau à large bord et ressortent à sa partie supérieure. La déformation du crâne et l'ornement en relief du front ainsi que le collier de perles et les bracelets sont les signes de son rang élevé. Un manteau lui enveloppe les épaules et le dos et dissimule la silhouette d'un vieux nain accroupi entre ses jambes.
Peinture bleue, rouge et blanche. Faite au moule, modelée à la main et suivant la technique du pastillage. Hauteur: 23 cm. Collection: Dr. Kurt Stavenhagen.

SEÑORA Y ENANO. La cabeza y el peinado sostienen un tocado de bandas de algodón entrelazadas, que están sujetas en su parte superior, a través de un sombrero de ala ancha, por cuya copa sale el entrelazado en forma de colgante. Presenta deformación craneana, aditamento en el nacimiento de la nariz y porta collar y pulseras de cuentas. El manto, que cubre la espalda, enmarca la figura de un viejo probablemente un enano, sentado entre sus piernas.
Conserva restos de pintura azul, roja y blanca. Hecha en molde, a mano libre y con técnica de pastillaje. Altura: 23 cm. Colección: Dr. Kurt Stavenhagen.

MÄNNLICHE FIGUR in ehrerbietiger Haltung. Sein eleganter Kopfschmuck besteht aus einer breiten, gefältelten Binde mit seitlichen
Verzierungen, darauf befindet sich ein Geflecht von Baumwollbändern,
die eine lose Schlinge bilden und von einem unsichtbaren Gestell ge-
stützt werden. Er hat einen deformierten Schädel und einen Nasenaufsatz. Die Ohrenscheiben, das Halsband und der Lendenschurz „ex"
vervollständigen seine einfache Bekleidung, die einen Kontrast bildet
zu der erlesenen Pracht seines Kopfputzes. Der Gegensatz wird noch
unterstrichen durch die plastische Sparsamkeit der Körperformen und
die reiche Ausdruckskraft der Gesichtszüge.
Blaue Farbreste. Handmodelliert und mit plastischen Auflagen versehen. Der Kopf ist vermutlich in der Form hergestellt. Höhe: 19,5 cm.
Sammlung: Stendahl.

MALE FIGURINE, in a reverent posture. His elegant head-dress is a
wide pleated band with lateral ornaments. Above, held in place by an
invisible frame, is a loop of twisted thick cotton cords, their ends hanging down like pendants. Skull deformation and addition to the nose.
Earplugs, a necklace and the "ex" complete his costume, the simplicity
of which contrasts with the splendour of his head-dress, a contrast
heightened by the simple shape of his body when compared with
the expressive features of his face.
Traces of blue paint. The head was probably molded, the body and
details hand-modeled and appliquéd. Height: 19.5 cm. Collection:
Stendahl.

FIGURINE MASCULINE, dans une attitude révérencielle. Son élégante
coiffure se compose d'un large bandeau garni d'ornements latéraux et
sur lequel repose un édifice de rubans de coton entrelacés en une
grosse boucle lâche, le tout soutenu par une armature invisible. Le
personnage a le crâne déformé et l'ornement nasal habituel. Les disques des oreilles, le collier et le pagne «ex» complètent sa tenue d'une
grande simplicité en contraste avec la splendeur raffinée de la coiffure.
On retrouve ce contraste également entre la richesse d'expression
du visage et la sobriété dans la facture du corps.
Traces de couleur rouges. Tête probablement faite au moule. Corps
et détails modelés suivant la technique du pastillage. Hauteur: 19,5 cm.
Collection: Stendahl.

FIGURILLA MASCULINA. En posición reverencial. Lleva un tocado elegante formado por una ancha banda plegada con adornos laterales.
Sobre la banda, sostenido por un armazón oculto, lleva un entrelazado
de gruesos cordones de algodón en forma de lazo abierto, cuyas
extremidades caen como colgantes. Acusa deformación craneana y
aditamento en la nariz. Las orejeras circulares, el collar de cordón y el
«ex» completan su sobria indumentaria que contrasta elegantemente
con la magnificencia del tocado, contribuyendo al feliz contraste
general entre la riqueza expresiva del rostro y la economía de las
formas del cuerpo.
Conserva restos de pintura azul. La cabeza probablemente fabricada
en molde. El cuerpo y los accesorios hechos a mano libre y con técnica
de pastillaje. Altura: 19,5 cm. Colección: Stendahl.

ZWERG. Ein ungestalter, fetter Hofnarr mit Schädeldeformation. Ein großer und komplizierter Turban aus Baumwolle, mit breiten, gefältelten Bändern und Rosetten verziert, bedeckt seinen Kopf. An der Nasenwurzel und auf dem Nasenrücken sind kleine Knötchen, die durch Hauteinschnitte hervorgerufen wurden. Zwei große Perlen bilden den Brustschmuck. Er trägt eine einfache Schambinde. Die oberste Rosette ist blau bemalt.

Die Figur ist eine Pfeife. In der Form hergestellt, handmodelliert, mit plastischen Auflagen versehen. Höhe: 15,5 cm. Sammlung Stendahl.

DWARF BUFFOON. A misshaped, fat body. An enormous and intricate cotton turban decorated with ribbons and rosettes covers his deformed head. On the ridge of his nose are beaded scars, and there is also a wedge-shaped scar between his brows. He wears round earplugs, and a breastplate of two globular beads. His "ex" has a small apron over his crossed feet.

The front rosette is painted blue. This figurine is a whistle, molded, hand-modeled and appliquéd. Height: 15.5 cm. Collection: Stendahl.

BOUFFON NAIN. Il est difforme et présente la déformation cranienne. Il est coiffé d'un volumineux turban de coton garni de larges rubans plissés et de rosettes. Il a sur l'arête et à la racine du nez des nodosités provenant d'incisions. Deux grandes perles composent son pectoral. Il ne porte qu'une étroite bande en guise de pagne «ex».

La rosette supérieure du turban est bleue. Figurine-sifflet, faite au moule et modelée à la main suivant la technique du pastillage. Hauteur: 15,5 cm. Collection: Stendahl.

ENANO BUFON. Deforme, obeso y con deformación craneana. La cabeza está cubierta con un elaborado y complicado turbante de algodón ornamentado de bandas y rosetones. Tiene una escoriación pequeña en el nacimiento de la nariz. Porta orejeras circulares y como pectoral dos cuentas. Tiene el «ex» ceñido en la cintura con banda al frente.

El rosetón en el frente está pintado de azul. Figurilla-silbato, hecha en molde, a mano libre y con pastillaje. Altura: 15,5 cm. Colección: Stendahl.

MÄNNLICHE FIGUR in ehrerbietiger Haltung. Um den Kopf ist ein Tuch geschlagen und mit einer dicken Schnur festgebunden. Zwei horizontal tatauierte Streifen in Mundhöhe verlaufen quer über das Gesicht. Ein breiter, geflochtener Gürtel mit langen Quasten hält den Lendenschurz „ex". In der linken Faust hat er einen runden Fächer aus geflochtenen Palmenblättern.
In der Form hergestellt. Höhe: 17 cm. Sammlung: Museo Nacional de Antropología, México.

MALE FIGURINE in reverent attitude. His head is covered with a scarf tied with a cord. Under a bulbous nose, two horizontal scarified lines cross from his mouth to his ears. His "ex" is held by a wide braided belt with long tassels. His left hand holds a woven circular palm fan.
Molded. Height: 17 cm. Collection: Museo Nacional de Antropología, Mexico.

FIGURINE MASCULINE, dans une attitude révérencielle. Sa tête est drapée dans une étoffe fixée par un gros cordon. Deux tatouages horizontaux lui barrent le visage au niveau de la bouche. Le pagne «ex»est maintenu par une large ceinture tressée garnie de longs pompons. Dans son poing gauche, il tient un éventail rond fait de feuilles de palmiers tressées.
Figurine faite au moule. Hauteur: 17 cm. Collection: Musée National d'Anthropologie, Mexico.

FIGURILLA MASCULINA. En actitud reverencial. Lleva un tocado de manto ceñido en la cabeza, anudado con grueso cordón. Presenta un tatuaje horizontal a la altura de la boca. Tiene el «ex» sostenido en la cintura por un ceñidor trenzado con borla al frente. En la mano izquierda empuña un abanico circular tejido de palma. Fabricada en molde.
Altura: 17 cm. Colección: Museo Nacional de Antropología, México.

KRIEGER. Über Haarbüscheln, die mit einer vorn zu einer Schleife ge-
bundenen, kräftigen Schnur verknüpft sind, trägt er eine Rundscheibe
aus Federn. Er zeigt Tatauierung und Knötchen auf Stirn, Kinn und
Mundwinkeln, hat einen Nasenaufsatz und Schädeldeformation. Ihn
schmücken Ohrscheiben, Halsband und als Brustschmuck eine Muschel. In der rechten Hand hält er den rechteckigen Schild der Mayas
und in der linken eine Schleuder für Steingeschosse.
Handmodelliert und mit plastischen Auflagen versehen. Der Kopf ist
vermutlich in der Form hergestellt. Höhe: 23 cm. Sammlung: Dr. Kurt
Stavenhagen.

WARRIOR. His hair is dressed in stiff spikes tied in front by a looped
cord and topped by a round crest of feathers. His deformed forehead
is covered with tattooed scars, and there are beaded scars on his chin
and at the corners of his mouth, besides the usual addition to the nose
at the brows. He wears earplugs, and a thick choker with a large shell
as a breastplate. In his right hand the rectangular Maya shield with a
fretted border, in his left a sling. His "ex" is a thick cotton cord tied
twice around his waist, with a short apron.
The head was probably molded, the body and details hand-modeled
and appliquéd. Height: 23 cm. Collection: Dr. Kurt Stavenhagen.

GUERRIER. Ses cheveux sont séparés et attachés par mèches à l'aide
d'un solide cordon qui fait une boucle sur le devant, et surmontés
d'un cercle de plumes. Il porte des tatouages, des nodosités sur le
front, le menton et aux commissures des lèvres ainsi que le «raccord»
nasal habituel. Son crâne est déformé. Il est paré de disques aux
oreilles, d'un collier et d'un pectoral qui est un grand coquillage. Il
tient dans sa main droite le bouclier rectangulaire des Mayas et dans la
gauche une fronde pour des projectiles de pierre.
Tête probablement faite au moule. Toute le reste modelé à la main et
au moyen de la technique du pastillage. Hauteur: 23 cm. Collection:
Dr. Kurt Stavenhagen.

GUERRERO. Lleva un tocado de rodela de plumas y guedejas anudadas
con grueso cordón y moño al frente. Presenta deformación craneana,
tatuaje de escoriaciones en la frente, en las comisuras de los labios y
en la barbilla y el aditamento usual sobre la nariz. Porta como ornamentos orejeras, collar de banda enrollada y pectoral de concha. En
la mano derecha empuña el escudo rectangular orlado y en la izquierda
la honda que se utilizaba para arrojar proyectiles de piedra.
La cabeza probablemente hecha en molde. El cuerpo y los accesorios
modelados a mano libre y aplicados mediante pastillaje. Altura: 23 cm.
Colección: Dr. Kurt Stavenhagen.

GEFANGENER, der unbekleidet ist und gepeinigt wurde. Das geschwollene linke Auge und der verzogene Mund verleihen ihm einen schmerzvollen Ausdruck. Auf der Stirn hat er eine künstliche Erhöhung.
Die Figur ist eine Rassel. In der Form hergestellt und mit plastischen Auflagen versehen. Höhe: 16 cm. Sammlung: Museo Nacional de Antropología, México.

NUDE PRISONER, who has been tortured. His left eye is swollen and his mouth contorted as if in pain. On his forehead a scarification as an addition to the nose.
This figurine is a rattle. Molded and appliquéd. Height: 16 cm. Collection: Museo Nacional de Antropología, Mexico.

CAPTIF nu, après une séance de torture. L'enflure de l'oeil gauche et la grimace de la bouche confèrent à son visage une expression douloureuse. Sur son front un ornement en relief.
Figurine-crécelle, faite au moule et d'après la technique du pastillage. Hauteur: 16 cm. Collection: Musée National d'Anthropologie, Mexico.

PRISIONERO DESNUDO. Ha sido atormentado. El ojo izquierdo está totalmente hinchado. La boca entreabierta y torcida le da la expresión de dolor. En la frente presenta una escoriación como aditamento de la nariz.
Figurilla-sonaja, hecha en molde y con pastillaje. Altura: 16 cm.

Colección: Museo Nacional de Antropología, México.

MÄNNLICHER KOPF. Der starke plastische und lebensnahe Ausdruck läßt vermuten, daß es sich um ein Porträt handelt. Die Schädeldeformation ist betont.
Vermutlich in der Form hergestellt. Höhe: 4 cm. Sammlung: Museo Reg. de Villahermosa, Tab.

MALE HEAD. The realistic and expressive features suggest a portrait. Remarkable skull deformation.
Probably molded. Height: 4 cm. Collection: Museo Reg. de Villahermosa, Tab.

TETE MASCULINE. Le réalisme et la vigueur de l'expression font supposer qu'il s'agit ici d'un portrait. La déformation cranienne est prononcée. Probablement faite au moule.
Hauteur: 4 cm environ. Collection: Musée Régional de Villahermosa, Tab.

CABEZA MASCULINA. La vigorosa expresión del modelado hace pensar en un retrato. Tiene deformación craneana muy notable.
Probablemente hecha en molde. Altura: 4 cm. Colección: Museo Reg.
de Villahermosa, Tab.

FRAU UND ZWERG. Auf der hohen Haartracht sitzt ein Hut mit breiter gezackter Krempe. Dicke Baumwollstreifen sind durch ihn hindurchgezogen. Der Schädel ist deformiert. Halb verborgen in ihrem weiten Mantel hockt ein Zwerg; vielleicht ein Diener.
Diese Sitzweise war wohl nicht sehr gebräuchlich bei den Mayas, denn meist sind die Figuren mit gekreuzten Beinen dargestellt.
Wenig Farbreste. In der Form hergestellt, handmodelliert und mit plastischen Auflagen versehen. Höhe: 21 cm. Privatsammlung.

WOMAN AND DWARF. On top of the hair-style is a hat with a wide jagged trim and a high cylindrical crown. Thick cotton-strands are pulled through it. Skull deformation. Half hidden by her wide cloak, a dwarf, perhaps a servant, is squatting below her crossed arms. A squatting figure is not often found among the Maya representations, their figures being mostly cross-legged.
Molded, hand-modeled and appliquéd. Height: 21 cm. Private Collection.

FEMME ET NAIN. La femme porte porte une haute coiffure surmontée d'un chapeau à large bord et qui est traversé par de grosses bandes de coton. Son crâne est déformé et son grand manteau dissimule à demi un nain accroupi, peut-être un serviteur.
Cette façon de s'asseoir était plutôt rare chez les Mayas qui généralement sont représentés assis en tailleur.
Quelques restes de peinture. Figurine taite au moule, modelée à la main et suivant la technique du pastillage. Hauteur: 21 cm. Collection privée.

SEÑORA Y ENANO. Ella lleva un alto peinado que señala la deformación craneana, cubierto de un sombrero de ancha ala orlada y alta copa rematada por una gruesa banda de algodón. Se adorna con orejeras y collar. Un largo manto cubre su espalda. El enano está sentado con las piernas flexionadas, posición poco común entre los mayas, que por lo general se sientan con las piernas cruzadas. Parece ser un sirviente.
Hecha en molde, a mano libre y con pastillaje. Conserva escasos restos de pintura. Altura: 21 cm. Colección: Particular.

JUNGES MÄDCHEN mit lebendigen und ausdrucksvollen Gesichts-zügen. Die Haartracht ist ein komplizierter Aufbau von Haarbüscheln und Strähnen. Eine große Kugel oder Perle ist ihr Nasenschmuck. Der bis zu den Brüsten reichende Rock wird von einem Gürtel zusammen-gehalten.
Handmodelliert und mit plastischen Auflagen versehen. Höhe: etwa 15 cm. Sammlung: Miguel Covarrubias.

YOUNG GIRL with lively and realistic features. Her hair is intricately arranged in tufts. She wears a spherical noseplug, bracelets and the "pic" covering her breasts.
Hand-modeled and appliquéd. Height: about 15 cm. Collection: Miguel Covarrubias.

JEUNE FILLE. Elle a une physiognomie vivante et expressive. Sa coiffure est une construction compliquée de touffes et de mèches de cheveux. Une grosse perle pare son nez. Sa tunique qui monte jus-qu'aux seins est retenue par une ceinture.
Figurine modelée à la main et suivant la technique du pastillage. Hauteur: 15 cm environ. Collection: Miguel Covarrubias.

DONCELLA. Sus rasgos son naturalistas y expresivos. Tiene un com-plicado peinado formado por guedejas, porta nariguera esférica, bra-zaletes y el «pic» que cubre desde los senos.
Modelada a mano libre con técnica de pastillaje. Altura: 15 cm aproxi-madamente. Colección: Miguel Covarrubias.

JUNGE FRAU UND GREIS. Die Frau trägt auf ihren Schultern einen lüsternen Greis, dessen Augenlider entzündet und angeschwollen sind; vielleicht ist er blind. Sie hat einen deformierten Schädel und das Haar ist geschmückt mit einer Blume. Eine Perlenschnur mit Quasten fällt über ihre Brust. Die Arme sind erhoben und halten den Alten. Dieser trägt einen Turban aus Baumwolle und ist in ein Gewand aus Baumwolle oder Fell gehüllt. Die rechte Hand hat er auf ihre Brust, die linke auf ihren Kopf gelegt.
Die Figur ist eine Rassel und in der Form hergestellt. Höhe: 15 cm. Sammlung: Museo Reg. de Campeche, Camp.

WOMAN AND OLD MAN. A girl carries a lustful old man on her shoulders. His eyes are closed, and his eyelids very swollen: perhaps he is blind. Her forehead is flattened and her hair is decorated with a flower. She wears earplugs and a beaded necklace, its tasseled ends hanging between her breasts. Her lifted arms hold the old man. He has a cotton turban, earplugs, a necklace and a breastplate, besides a "buc", a cotton or monkey-skin dress. With his right hand he holds on to the woman's breast, with the left to her head.
This figurine is a rattle, molded. Height: 15 cm. Collection: Museo Reg. de Campeche, Camp.

JEUNE FILLE ET VIEILLARD. La femme porte sur ses épaules un vieillard lubrique dont les paupières sont enflammées et gonflées. Peut-être même est-il aveugle. Elle a le crâne déformé et la chevelure décorée d'une fleur. Un collier de perles à pompons lui tombe sur la poitrine. Ses bras sont levés et tiennent le vieillard. Celui-ci porte un turban de coton et un vêtement également de coton ou de fourrure. Sa main droite est posée sur la poitrine de la femme et sa main gauche sur sa tête.
Figurine-crécelle, faite au moule. Hauteur: 15 cm. Collection: Musée Régional de Campeche, Camp.

MUJER Y ANCIANO. Doncella que carga sobre sus hombros a un anciano lascivo, de párpados exageradamente hinchados y cerrados, quizás un ciego. Ella presenta deformación craneana. El peinado está adornado con una flor. Porta collar de cuentas, que cae sobre su pecho. Con los brazos hacia arriba sostiene al anciano. Este lleva un turbante de algodón, orejeras, collar y pectoral. Viste el «buc» o vestido de algodón o de piel de mono. Apoya la mano derecha sobre el seno de la mujer y la izquierda sobre su cabeza.
Figurilla-sonaja, hecha en molde. Altura: 15 cm. Colección: Museo Reg.
de Campeche, Camp.

ALTE FRAU. Sie trägt ein Kind (Kopf fehlt) mit einem Schal auf den Rücken gebunden. So, wie es die eingeborenen Frauen noch heute tun. Auf dem Kopf trägt sie ein Tuch und darüber ein Tragpolster. Die gestutzten Haare fallen auf die Stirn. Die Gesichtszüge sind naturalistisch und lassen die typischen Alterserscheinungen, Falten und zahnloser Mund, besonders hervortreten. Sie trägt Ohrpflöcke, Halskette und die Bluse „kub" und den Rock „pic". In den Händen hält sie ein kleines Räuchergefäß. Hier ist eine einfache Frau aus dem Volke dargestellt.

Die Figur ist eine Rassel. In der Form hergestellt, handmodelliert. Höhe: 15 cm. Sammlung: Museo Reg. de Campeche, Camp.

OLD WOMAN. She carries a child in a shawl on her back, just as the natives do nowadays. The child's head is missing. Under a thick padded ring on top of her head, a scarf and a straight-cut fringe of hair frame her face. Large earplugs, a necklace, the "kub" and the "pic" constitute her attire. She holds an incense burner on her crossed legs. She portrays the common native woman.

This figurine is a rattle. Molded, hand-modeled. Height: 15 cm. Collection: Museo Reg. de Campeche, Camp.

FEMME AGEE. Elle porte un enfant (dont la tête est manquante) attaché sur son dos par un fichu, comme c'est encore l'usage aujourd'hui chez les femmes indigènes. Elle a sur la tête un foulard sur lequel repose un coussinet. Ses cheveux coupés courts tombent en frange sur son front. Les traits du visage sont pleins de réalisme et la décrépitude de l'âge, les rides et la bouche édentée sont rendues de façon particulièrement frappante. Elle est parée de disques d'oreilles ainsi que d'un collier de perles et vêtue de la blouse «kub» et de la jupe «pic». Elle tient dans ses mains un petit encensoir. Il s'agit ici d'une simple femme du peuple.

Figurine-crécelle, faite au moule et modelée suivant la technique du pastillage: Hauteur: 15 cm. Collection: Musée Régional de Campeche, Camp.

ANCIANA. Carga con un lienzo al infante (falta la cabeza) sobre la espalda, como aún se usa entre las indígenas. Lleva la cabeza ceñida por un manto anudado con grueso rodete y en la frente caen los flecos de cabellos recortados. Los rasgos faciales son muy naturalistas, lo que acusan las arrugas y la boca desdentada. Porta orejeras, collar y la camisa «kub» y la falda «pic». En las manos sostiene un incensario. Esta figurilla representa la mujer del pueblo.

Figurilla-sonaja, hecha en molde y a mano libre. Altura: 15 cm. Colección: Museo Reg. de Campeche, Camp.

JÜNGLING. Ein Schreiber oder Musikant, der etwas in eine Tafel ritzt oder auf einem Instrument spielt. Der Kopfschmuck ist aus einem Tuch und geflochtenen Bändern gearbeitet, die auf den Nacken fallen. Der Lendenschurz ,,ex" ist auf den Hüften verknotet.
Die Figur ist rot bemalt. In der Form hergestellt, handmodelliert und mit plastischen Auflagen versehen. Höhe: etwa 15 cm. Sammlung: Dr. Kurt Stavenhagen.

YOUNG MAN. A scribe or a musician with an instrument on his lap. His head-dress consists of braided bands, their ends falling on the nape of his neck. His "ex" is knotted in front.
Molded, hand-modeled and appliquéd. Height: about 15 cm. Collection: Dr. Kurt Stavenhagen.

ADOLESCENT. La figurine représente un scribe ou un musicien qui grave une tablette ou joue d'un instrument. Sa coiffure est faite d'une étoffe et de rubans tressés, qui retombent sur la nuque. Le pagne «ex» est noué sur les hanches.
La figurine est peinte en rouge. Faite au moule, modelée à la main suivant la technique du pastillage. Hauteur: 15 cm environ. Collection: Dr. Kurt Stavenhagen.

ADOLESCENTE. Escriba o músico que tañe un instrumento. Porta el tocado elaborado de bandas trenzadas que caen sobre la nuca y el «ex» anudado en la cintura.
Está pintado de rojo. Hecho en molde, a mano libre y con técnica de pastillaje. Altura: 15 cm. aproxidamente. Colección: Dr. Stavenhagen.

GEFÄSS in Gestalt einer menschlichen Figur, die wahrscheinlich einen Musikanten darstellt. Es scheint, daß er mit der rechten Hand auf einem runden Instrument spielt. Den Kopfschmuck bildet ein Tierkopf, vielleicht ein Lama. Der Anhänger an der Vorderseite dient ihm als verlängerter Nasenrücken. Der Schädel ist deformiert. Der Brustschmuck ist eine zylindrische Perle.

Rote, weiße und blaue Farbreste. In der Form hergestellt, handmodelliert und mit plastischen Auflagen versehen. Höhe 18 cm. Sammlung: Carlos Pellicer.

EFFIGY VESSEL, probably representing a musician. He seems to be playing with his right hand on a round instrument. His headdress has the shape of an animal's head, possibly a llama's. A tassel on his forehead takes the place of the addition to his nose. Skull deformation. A cylindrical head forms his gorget.

Traces of red, blue and white paint. Molded, hand-modeled and appliquéd. Height: 18 cm. Collection: Carlos Pellicer.

VASE-PORTRAIT. Le personnage est sans doute un musicien car il semble jouer de la main droite sur un instrument circulaire. Son chapeau représente une tête d'animal, probablement un lama, et il est garni sur l'avant d'une pendeloque qui lui prolonge en même temps l'arête nasale. Son crâne est déformé. Il porte un pectoral fait d'une grande perle cylindrique.

Traces de couleur rouge et bleue. Fait au moule et modelé suivant la technique du pastillage. Hauteur: 18 cm. Collection: Carlos Pellicer.

VASIJA. En forma de figurilla; representa probablemente un músico. Parece que con la mano derecha tañe un instrumento circular. Lleva el tocado formado por un animal, tal vez una llama, con colgante al frente, que le sirve como aditamento en el nacimiento de la nariz. Como pectoral trae una gran cuenta cilíndrica.

Conserva restos de pintura roja, blanca y azul. Hecha en molde, a mano libre y con pastillaje. Altura: 18 cm. Colección: Carlos Pellicer.

HUND. Schon in früher Zeit war der Hund in Amerika ein Haustier und wurde auch gegessen. Er trägt ein Cape mit Halskrause und Schleife. Blaue Farbreste.
Die Figur ist eine Pfeife und in der Form hergestellt. Höhe: 15,5 cm. Sammlung: Stendahl.

DOG. Since early time, the dog has been domesticated and used for food. It wears a cape with a ruff tied with a bow in front.
Traces of blue paint. This figurine is a whistle, molded. Height: 15.5 cm. Collection: Stendahl.

CHIEN. Le chien était considéré en Amérique déjà dans les temps anciens comme animal domestique et également comme chair comestible. Il porte une cape à collerette avec un noeud.
Traces de couleur bleue. Figurine-sifflet faite au moule. Hauteur: 15,5 cm. Collection: Stendahl.

PERRO. Desde los primeros tiempos americanos aparece el perro domesticado, que además servía como alimento. Porta una capa con gorguera y moño al frente.
Conserva restos de pintura azul. Figurilla-silbato, fabricada en molde.
Altura: 15,5 cm. Colección: Stendahl.

PRIESTER. Der weite Mantel und die Gürtelschließe, die einen Toten-
kopf darstellt, kennzeichnen ihn als einen dem Totenkult geweihten
Priester. Auf seinem deformierten Schädel trug er ursprünglich einen
abnehmbaren Kopfschmuck. Großer Scheibenohrschmuck mit Ge-
hänge, ein Brustschmuck in Schmetterlingsform und ein ausgezackter
Lendenschurz „ex" schmücken und kleiden ihn.
Handmodelliert und mit plastischen Auflagen versehen. Höhe: 13,5 cm.
Sammlung: Dr. Kurt Stavenhagen.

PRIEST. His wide cape and the buckle of his "ex" in the shape of a
skull identify him as a priest of the death cult. His shaved head is
excessively deformed. The plumed head-dress, presumably removable,
is missing. He wears large ear ornaments with pendants, and a collar
of thick cords which support a magnificent breastplate picturing a
butterfly. The kilt-like loincloth is cut in fringes.
Hand-modeled and appliquéd. Height: 13.5 cm. Collection: Dr. Kurt
Stavenhagen.

PRETRE. Son ample manteau et la boucle de sa ceinture qui représente
une tête de mort indiquent qu'il s'agit d'un prêtre consacré au culte
des morts. Il portait à l'origine sur son crâne déformé une coiffure
de plumes amovible. Il est paré de grands disques d'oreilles à pendeloques et d'un pectoral en forme de papillon et il est habillé d'un pagne
«ex» à dentelures.
Figurine modelée à la main d'après la technique du pastillage. Hauteur:
13,5 cm. Collection: Dr. Kurt Stavenhagen.

SACERDOTE. El manto que cubre su espalda y el broche del «ex», en
forma de cráneo, lo caracterizan como sacerdote del culto de los
muertos. La cabeza rapada acusa deformación craneana. Porta orejeras circulares con largos colgantes y un collar de grueso cordón
sostiene un magnífico pectoral en forma de mariposa. El borde del
«ex» está recortado en flecos. Le falta el tocado de plumas que seguramente era desmontable.
Modelado a mano libre con técnica de pastillaje. Altura: 13,5 cm.
Colección: Dr. Kurt Stavenhagen.

HOHER PRIESTER UND WÜRDENTRÄGER „HALACH UINIC". Er sitzt auf einem Jaguarthron auf einer Plattform, zu der eine Stufe führt. Der obere Teil des Thronhimmels ist mit einer Fratze geschmückt, die eine Regengottheit mit Federbusch und Diadem darstellt. Sie hat Augenringe und Fangzähne, die bezeichnend sind für die nahuatl Gottheit „Tlaloc". Wir dürfen daher annehmen, daß diese Figur aus einer späten Kulturepoche der Mayas stammt. Der Priester trägt einen Kopfschmuck aus drei Federbündeln, die Flügel und Schwanz eines Vogels symbolisieren. Ihn schmücken Perlenschnüre, Ohrscheiben und Armreifen. Die Betonung der Horizontalen in Basis und Architrav sind auf den kulturellen Einfluß aus dem nördlichen Hochland zurückzuführen. Der Jaguarthron ist dagegen typisch Maya.
In der Form hergestellte Rassel. Höhe 23 cm. Privatsammlung.

HIGH PRIEST AND DIGNITARY "HALACH UINIC". He is seated on a throne shaped like a jaguar, on a platform with a step in the center. The canopy is topped by an enormous mask representing a rain god with a plume crest and diadem. The deity has fangs and rings around the eyes, typical features of the Nahuatl god "Tlaloc", which indicate a late date in Maya culture for the piece. The priest has a headdress of three bundles of feathers forming a bird's wings and tail. He wears earplugs, necklaces, wristlets and the "ex". The predominance of the horizontal lines in the base and crossbar of the throne denotes the influence of the Northern Plateau, but the jaguar throne is typicaly Mayan.
This figurine is a rattle, molded. Height: 23 cm. Private Collection.

GRAND PRÊTRE ET DIGNITAIRE «HALACH UINIC». Il est assis sur la plateforme d'un thrône en forme de jaguar à laquelle on accède par une marche. La partie supérieure du dais est décorée d'un visage grimaçant représentant une divinité de la pluie coiffée d'un panache de plumes et d'un diadème. Les yeux entourés de cercles et la bouche garnie de crocs sont les caractéristiques de la divinité nahuatl «Tlaloc», ce qui laisse supposer que cette figurine se rattache à une époque récente de l'art maya. Le grand-prêtre est coiffé de trois plumets qui symbolisent les ailes et la queue d'un oiseau. Il porte plusieurs rangs de perles, des disques aux oreilles et des bracelets. L'accentuation de l'horizontale dans la base et l'architrave est due à l'influence du haut-plateau nordique tandis que le thrône-jaguar est, lui, typiquement maya.
Figurine-crécelle faite au moule. Hauteur: 23 cm. Collection privée.

GRAN SEÑOR «HALACH UINIC». Está sentado en un trono en forma de jaguar sobre una plataforma en cuyo centro se ve un escalón. El dosel está decorado en la parte superior con un gran mascarón, que representa a una deidad de la lluvia, con un penacho de plumas ceñido por una diadema. La deidad lleva anteojeras, dientes y colmillos característicos de la divinidad nahuatl «Tlaloc», y por tanto tardía en la cultura maya. El Gran Señor lleva un tocado hecho con atados de plumas, que forman las alas y la cola de un ave. Porta collares, orejeras, pulseras y el «ex». La relación horizontal de la base y la trave superior es también influencia del altiplano, pero el tema del trono jaguar es típico maya.

Figurilla-sonaja, hecha en molde. Altura: 23 cm. Colección: Particular.